MEANING
OVER
PURPOSE

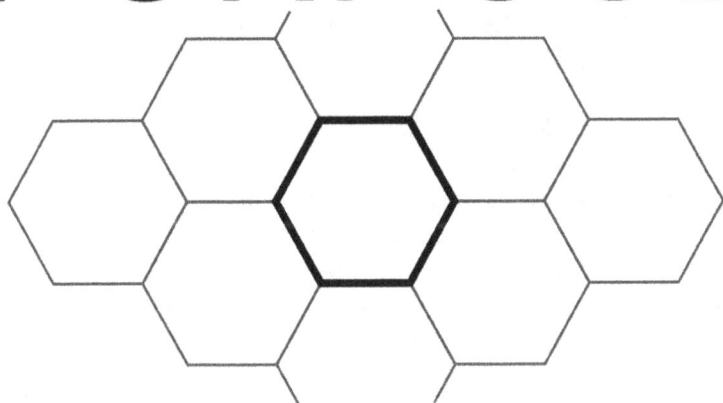

The CEO's strategic
blueprint for growth and
lasting engagement

ANGELA RIXON

EU GPSR representative: LOGOS EUROPE, 9 rue Nicolas Poussin, LA ROCHELLE 17000, France Contact@logoseurope.eu

Want to bulk-buy copies of this book for your team and colleagues? We can customize the content and co-brand *Meaning Over Purpose* to suit your business's needs.

Please email info@practicalinspiration.com for more details.

Practical Inspiration
Publishing

Contents

List of figures

Introduction:
The Hexagon – your
strategic map for
meaningful work

'The purpose of life is not to be happy. It is to be useful,
to be honorable, to be compassionate, to have it make
some difference that you have lived and lived well.'
Ralph Waldo Emerson

The meaning gap – why we're losing the battle for engagement

Emerson's sobering words feel more relevant now than ever before.

We stand at a crossroads in leadership. In boardrooms around the world, senior executives are asking a familiar question: *How do we retain our best people and unlock the energy required to grow when the rules of work are changing?*

And they are changing.

Today's employees are not only working harder, but they're also asking deeper questions. They want to know their efforts matter. They want to feel aligned, not just with the company's goals, but with who they are as people: their strengths, values, and interests. And more than ever they want their work to mean something – not in a vague philosophical sense, but in real, daily terms.

Despite visionary strategies and significant investment in culture and engagement, something critical is missing.

Only 21% of employees globally are thriving at work

According to Gallup (2024), four out of five employees say they feel disconnected from their organization's mission and values.

The data is clear: burnout, attrition and 'quiet quitting' are not anomalies – they are symptoms.

We're not just facing a purpose gap; we're facing a meaning gap

This book begins with a bold idea: meaning is not a soft ambition. It is your next strategic advantage. Without meaning, purpose feels hollow. Culture becomes fragile. Engagement becomes performative.

This book introduces the Meaning Over Purpose blueprint – a practical, proven system for closing what I call the Purpose-to-Meaning Gap: the disconnect between what an organization says and what its people actually feel. *(Use Appendix 1: Meaning Gap Self-diagnostic Tool to assess this in your organization.)*

In Figure 1, the Purpose-to-Meaning Gap provides a visual representation of how purpose becomes disconnected from daily experience – and why meaning must be incorporated into the everyday.

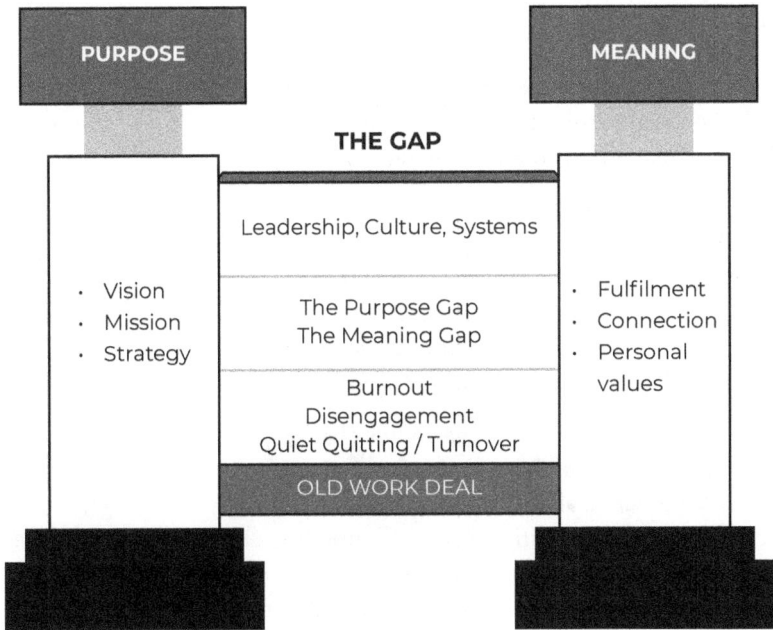

Figure 1: Many organizations have a bold purpose statement, but that purpose is often disconnected from employees' day-to-day experiences. The result is the Purpose-to-Meaning Gap where values are declared but not felt. Closing the gap requires leadership that activates meaning at every level, not just strategy from the top.

Why I wrote this book

I've worked in organizations where the purpose statement was inspiring – genuinely, goosebump-worthy stuff. 'Changing the world.' 'Powering a better future.' But behind the glossy words, I saw something quite different: toxic cultures, performative leadership and people quietly burning out or opting out altogether. What they said didn't match what they did. That 'say-do' gap wasn't just uncomfortable – it was corrosive. It made me question everything I thought I knew about what work was supposed to feel like.

For years, I did what many of us do: I worked hard, climbed the ladder and chased what success looked like on paper. And there were glimmers – exciting projects, managers who genuinely supported my growth, brilliant individuals and energizing teams. But if I'm brutally honest, those experiences were in the minority. More often, I found myself surrounded by behaviour I didn't trust, in environments that didn't reflect my values. I realized I wanted more than a salary or a job title. I wanted to solve meaningful problems, grow as a person and create spaces where others could do the same.

When I stepped into leadership, I knew I didn't want to do it the old way. I believed you could drive performance through people, not despite them; that being human at work didn't weaken a leader's edge, it strengthened it. Later, as a change leader, I had the opportunity to test that belief by designing programmes that brought people in, rather than pushing change at them. Project Morpheus was one of those.

Project Morpheus was a behavioural change programme designed to engage the hearts and minds of the workforce at a global technology firm. While service level agreements were technically being met, clients remained dissatisfied citing a lack of innovation and value. The initiative shifted focus from contract compliance to true client centricity and everyday innovation, encouraging employees to think beyond the metrics and deliver meaningful, value-adding outcomes. It delivered business results: a five-fold increase in client satisfaction, the renewal of a significant client contract worth $50 million and a deeply engaged workforce – proof that meaning isn't just a moral good, it's a strategic lever.

This book brings together three decades of lived experience and evidence-based research – including a year studying Applied Positive Psychology and Coaching Psychology – and hundreds of research and coaching conversations with leaders, teams and change agents who all want the same thing: a better way to work, one that fuels business success *and* personal sustainability. One where people thrive, not just survive.

I wrote this book for anyone who has felt the quiet (or not-so-quiet) ache of disconnection at work. For leaders who want to do the right thing but are under pressure to deliver results. For the people who don't fit the outdated 'ideal worker' model. And for the organizations ready to make space for a new kind of leadership.

I am a champion of meaningful work because it delivers human fulfilment, unlocks untapped potential and drives extraordinary business results. It's not a quick fix, but it is one of the most transformational levers a leader can pull.

'Meaning' isn't a soft word for soft people – it's your sharpest edge. And it may be the most human-centric strategy you will ever pursue.

Introducing a new system for embedding meaning

Across decades of research and practice, one truth has emerged repeatedly: people don't leave companies. They leave experiences that feel empty, misaligned or meaningless. And often, they leave despite a compelling purpose.

That's why I and my colleagues at The Centre for Meaningful Work created the Meaning Over Purpose blueprint – a new system for embedding meaning into the DNA of your organization.

It's not a set of values; it's not a cultural campaign. It's a leadership operating system that enables meaning to become measurable, sustainable and scalable.

Figure 2 shows how the blueprint works. It integrates three proprietary frameworks into one cohesive system for driving culture and performance. The system is made up of three integrated elements:

The Meaningful Work Hexagon

The Meaningful Work Hexagon defines the six strategic capabilities required to embed meaning at scale: Purpose and Direction, Personal Meaning, Meaningful Leadership, Meaningful Culture, Measurable Impact and Systemic Sustainability.

The Meaningful Work sub-frameworks

The sub-frameworks define what must be built and measured to make meaning real. These include:

- The Five Pillars of Meaningful Work (Autonomy, Mastery, Purpose, Connection, Impact)

- The Lead with Meaning playbook (everyday leadership habits)

- Meaning Metrics (dashboard for Alignment, Growth, Connection and Resonance)

- The Culture Carrier model (strategies for scaling through people)

- The Legacy Design Loop (succession and sustainability over time)

The Meaningful Work Ecosystem

The Meaningful Work Ecosystem operationalizes how meaning is embedded across the system at the individual, team, leader and organizational levels. It links culture design to routines, leadership behaviours, systems and structures.

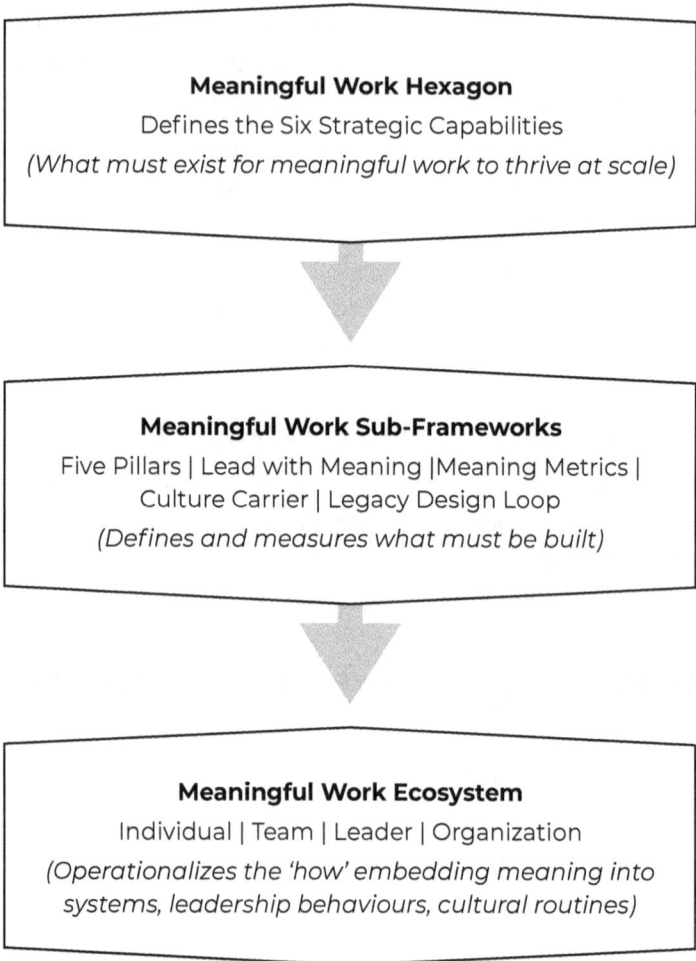

Meaningful Work Hexagon

Defines the Six Strategic Capabilities

(What must exist for meaningful work to thrive at scale)

Meaningful Work Sub-Frameworks

Five Pillars | Lead with Meaning |Meaning Metrics | Culture Carrier | Legacy Design Loop

(Defines and measures what must be built)

Meaningful Work Ecosystem

Individual | Team | Leader | Organization

(Operationalizes the 'how' embedding meaning into systems, leadership behaviours, cultural routines)

Figure 2: The Meaning Over Purpose blueprint closes the Purpose-to-Meaning Gap by integrating three components – six strategic capabilities, five sub-frameworks and ecosystem layers – which form a repeatable system for scaling meaningful work.

The six strategic capabilities to embed meaning at scale

To embed meaningful work at scale, leaders need more than positive intent. They need a system with clearly defined capabilities, supported by robust frameworks and reinforced through behaviour and structure.

Figure 3 shows the Meaningful Work Hexagon, the integrative visual for the Meaning Over Purpose blueprint. It outlines the six strategic capabilities which organizations must build to close the Purpose-to-Meaning Gap and sustain meaning over time:

- Purpose and Direction – aligning vision, goals and meaning

- Personal Meaning – enabling individual alignment and fulfilment

- Meaningful Leadership – translating culture through daily behaviour

- Meaningful Culture – designing systems that scale connection, impact and belonging

- Measurable Impact – using data to protect what matters

- Systemic Sustainability – ensuring meaning endures across generations, roles and business cycles

These six capabilities are supported by five core sub-frameworks. Together, they form a repeatable strategy for culture and leadership development to ensure meaning is not left to chance. Rather, it's designed, embedded and reinforced.

The Meaning Over Purpose blueprint equips leaders with the clarity, behaviours and systems required to embed meaningful work at scale. But its true power lies in what it unlocks: a new kind of leadership. One that doesn't separate performance from humanity. One that doesn't treat culture as an initiative, but as the engine of performance.

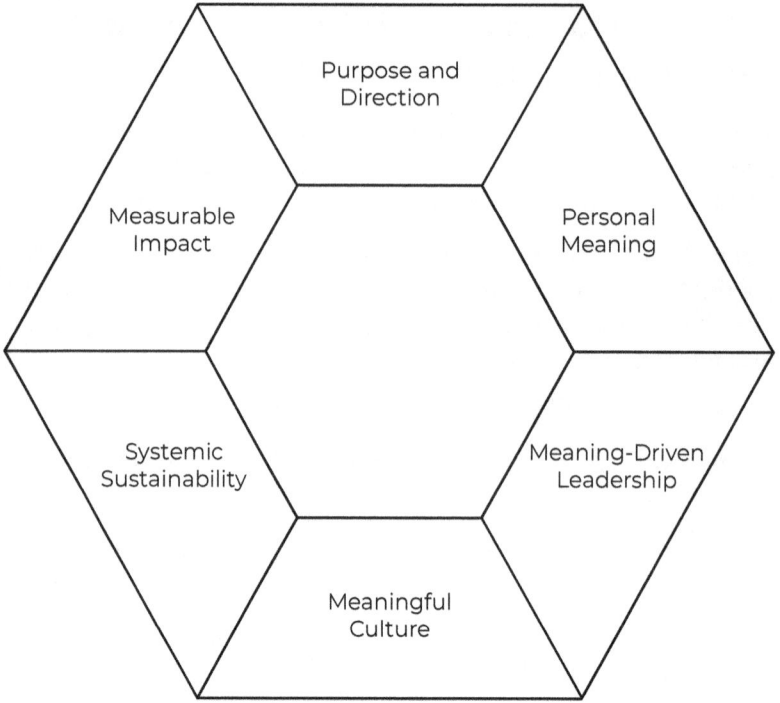

Figure 3: The Meaningful Work Hexagon visualizes the six core capabilities of the Meaning Over Purpose blueprint. Clockwise from the top: Purpose and Direction, Personal Meaning, Meaningful Leadership, Meaningful Culture, Measurable Impact and Systemic Sustainability.

A movement for the future of leadership

What began as a research inquiry has become something more: a growing movement of leaders – CEOs, people leaders, culture builders – who are reimagining what business can be. They understand that meaning is not a luxury.

It's how we fuel sustainable performance.

It's how we retain great people.

It's how we unlock energy, creativity, loyalty and growth – not just for employees, but for customers and communities.

The Meaning Over Purpose movement is not a trend. It's the new baseline for leaders who believe that business can serve people and that people can drive business.

This book is for you if:

- You are a CEO or executive leader navigating growth, change or disengagement.

- You are a culture builder, HR or transformation lead, seeking practical tools that scale.

- You are a manager, team leader or coach who knows there is more to give and more to build.

- You want to measure culture without reducing it.

- You want to lead with meaning but don't want to lose your edge.

This is not a soft book for soft leaders. It's a strategic guide to the hardest, most human part of leadership:

Creating organizations where people don't just stay – they thrive.

Where culture doesn't just inspire – it performs.

Where meaning isn't a side effect – it's the strategy.

The book begins with Sarah – a fictional CEO whose journey reflects the reality of thousands of leaders I've coached, studied, or advised. As she wrestles with growth, pressure and legacy, she uncovers what it means to lead with meaning – and how to embed that meaning so deeply that culture becomes a competitive advantage and a personal legacy.

This book won't give you all the answers.

But it will give you the map. And the models. And the questions that matter.

The movement has already begun. The question is no longer *if* you'll lead culture. The question is *how* you'll lead it – and what you'll leave behind when you do.

Theoretical underpinnings

Before we dive into the stories, strategies and systems that make up this book, it's important to identify the deeper research that underpins the Meaning Over Purpose blueprint. This has been built on decades of evidence from organizational science, psychology, motivation theory and leadership research. Each of the blueprint's three interlocking components is supported by its own body of theory and practice.

1. The Meaningful Work Hexagon

This defines the six strategic capabilities (Purpose and Direction, Personal Meaning, Meaningful Leadership, Meaningful Culture, Measurable Impact and Systemic Sustainability) required to embed meaningful work at scale. These capabilities are informed by integrative models from:

- Organizational culture and leadership (Schein, 2010)

- Systems thinking and sustainability (Meadows, 2008; Bronfen-brenner, 1977)

- Positive organizational scholarship (Cameron and Spreitzer, 2012)

- Legacy and identity frameworks (Ibarra, 2003; Shamir and Eilam, 2005)

- Strategic measurement models (Kaplan and Norton, 1996)

2. The Meaningful Work sub-frameworks

These define what must be built and measured to embed meaning in practice.

The Five Pillars of Meaningful Work (Autonomy, Mastery, Purpose, Connection and Impact)

Drawn from core theories of motivation and meaning, including:

- Self-determination theory (Deci and Ryan, 2000), which identifies autonomy, competence (mastery) and relatedness (connection) as core psychological needs that drive intrinsic motivation.

- Job characteristics theory (Hackman and Oldham (1976), which shows that task significance, skills variety and autonomy contribute to experienced meaningfulness.

- Prosocial motivation (Grant, 2007) and calling orientation (Wrzesniewski et al., 1997), which demonstrate that seeing the impact of your work – especially on others – significantly increases meaning and motivation.

The Lead with Meaning playbook is a leadership behaviour model grounded in:

- Servant leadership (Greenleaf, 1977)

- Authentic leadership (George, 2003; Avolio and Gardner, 2005)

- Emotional intelligence (Goleman, 1998)

- Level 5 leadership (Collins, 2005)

- The Progress Principle (Amabile and Kramer, 2011), especially the value of small wins and visible growth. Together, these insights provide the foundation for a practical, behavioural standard that leaders at any level can learn, model and sustain.

Meaning Metrics model is a new dashboard for culture drawing from:

- Engagement psychology (Saks, 2006)

- Work and meaning inventory (Steger et al., 2012)

- Employee recognition, wellbeing and emotional culture studies (Fisher, 2010; McKee, 2014)

- The balanced scorecard (Kaplan and Norton, 1996), which opened the door for integrating non-financial metrics into business strategy

Its four core domains of Alignment, Growth, Connection and Resonance reflect the psychological, emotional and social dimensions that sustain performance, not just sentiment.

The Culture Carrier model

Emerging from both practice and theory on:

- Informal leadership and social networks (Cross and Parker, 2004)

- Role modelling and influence (Bandura, 1986)

- Cultural transmission and storytelling (Denison, 1990; Schein, 2010)

The Legacy Design Loop

Built on frameworks of:

- Leader identity work and career transitions (Ibarra, 2003; Hall and Chandler, 2005)

- Succession and system continuity (Zenger and Folkman, 2009)

- Sustainable leadership (Hargreaves and Fink, 2006)

3. The Meaningful Work Ecosystem

This component operationalizes how meaning is embedded at every level of the organization from individual experience to team dynamics, leadership behaviour and systemic structures. The ecosystem is rooted in multi-level thinking, including:

- Ecological systems theory (Bronfenbrenner, 1977), which identifies that individuals are shaped by layered systems – an insight that applies to organizations and the experience of work.

- Organizational design and alignment – Galbraith's 2002 Star Model shows that meaningful work is sustained when strategy, structure, process, rewards and people are aligned.

- Organizational culture and leadership (Schein, 2010), reinforcing the need for alignment between personal values, leadership behaviours and structural design.

- Positive organizational scholarship (Cameron and Spreitzer, 2012), which affirms that purpose, trust and wellbeing are scalable performance drivers.

Together, these three components – capabilities, sub-frameworks and ecosystem layers – form the foundation of the Meaning Over Purpose blueprint: a system built not just to inspire meaning, but to embed and sustain it at scale.

PART I

THE QUEST FOR GROWTH IN A CHANGING WORLD

Sarah had always believed in the power of growth: revenue, market share, talent acquisition, efficiency. These were the metrics she'd been trained to pursue. The language she'd learned to speak. As a CEO, her role had been to deliver results – and she had. Year after year, NexusNova had grown stronger on paper.

But quietly, beneath the performance dashboards and strategy decks, a new kind of tension had begun to surface.

It started with unease. A sense that engagement wasn't as strong as it seemed. That retention was dipping not just because of competition, but because something deeper wasn't landing. Conversations with colleagues grew shorter. Eyes stopped lighting up. And the word 'purpose' – once energizing – began to feel hollow.

Then came the moment that changed everything.

A team leader, loyal and talented, raised his hand in a meeting and said:

'I understand the strategy. But I don't feel connected to it. Are we really doing something that matters?'

Sarah couldn't shake that question. Because she'd been asking it too, in her own way.

That's where this journey begins. Not with burnout. Not with crisis. But with the brave discomfort of a leader ready to ask more of herself and her organization.

This first part of the book lays the foundation for what comes next. Together, through Sarah's story and my research depicted through the executive coach and consultant Angela in the fictional story, we'll explore:

- Why purpose alone isn't enough to create engagement that lasts

- How today's leadership playbooks are failing to meet the emotional and generational needs of the workforce

- What happens when the contract between employer and employee no longer feels human

- Why meaningful work – once considered a soft ideal – is now emerging as one of the most important growth strategies of the coming decades

This is not a story about performance versus people. It's about what happens when performance depends on people – and when people are asking for something more.

Welcome to Part I: The quest for growth in a changing world.

Chapter 1
The wake-up call – becoming a meaning-driven CEO

'Ever more people today have the means to live, but
no meaning to live for.'
Viktor Frankl

Summary

In this opening chapter, we meet Sarah McKinnon, CEO of NexusNova, as she faces a quiet but critical leadership reckoning. Despite her company's strong sense of purpose on paper, employees are increasingly disconnected in practice. An eye-opening leadership meeting and a candid coaching session reveal a deeper issue – not just a purpose gap, where company purpose feels abstract, but a more personal, emotional void: a meaning gap, where people no longer feel their work matters to them (Kahn, 1990; Bloom, 2018).

Together, these create what we call the Purpose-to-Meaning Gap – the disconnect between what an organization *says* and what its people *feel*. When this gap goes unaddressed, performance suffers, disengagement rises and the company quietly loses its cultural anchor (Gallup, 2023; Baumeister, 1991).

This is not a fringe concern. Gallup's 2024 report shows that just 21% of employees globally feel engaged at work – and a majority report disconnection from their organization's purpose (Gallup, 2024). Meanwhile, the personal toll of meaninglessness in work is well documented. Baumeister (1991) described this as an 'existential vacuum' – a slow erosion of fulfilment that drains motivation, even in otherwise successful professionals.

Through Sarah's story and supporting research, Chapter 1 reframes meaningful work not as a 'nice-to-have', but as a strategic imperative. Purpose alone is not enough to sustain engagement – it must be activated through daily, emotionally resonant experiences of meaning. That is what unlocks innovation, resilience and long-term performance (McKinsey and Company, 2021; Luthans, Youssef and Avolio, 2007).

Sarah's wake-up call

Sarah McKinnon tapped her pen gently against her notebook, a habit that soothed her nerves during tense boardroom meetings. Today wasn't a negotiation or a routine update – it was supposed to be a celebration. Her senior leadership team sat around the expansive NexusNova boardroom table in London, having just reviewed another quarter of solid results. Yet an odd silence stretched across the room.

She cleared her throat. 'Is there anything else before we wrap up?' she prompted, expecting only routine questions. To her surprise, Tariq – a dynamic team lead known for his candour – hesitated, then raised his hand.

'I hope this isn't out of place,' he began cautiously, 'but lately I've found it increasingly hard to connect my everyday responsibilities to what we say our bigger mission is – powering the platforms that shape the future and help every person thrive. I understand the words. I know the strategy. But honestly, on a day-to-day basis, it just feels a bit… abstract.'

A ripple of discomfort passed through the room. A few people shuffled papers; someone cleared their throat. Sarah noticed Leonie, the head of HR, looking up from her notes and meeting her eyes. Leonie's concerned expression quietly communicated what Sarah already suspected: *We've been here before.*

Sarah composed herself, then addressed Tariq with a careful warmth. 'I appreciate your honesty, Tariq. It's important we speak openly. Can you say more about what's disconnecting for you?'

Tariq nodded. 'It's not outright dissatisfaction. It's more subtle – a feeling of disconnection. We've won awards for our culture and innovation, which is great. But some of us just don't feel our daily contributions link to the vision we promote externally. We say we're shaping the future, but are we really? Are we changing anything that matters to us personally?'

His words hung in the air – a challenge no one could immediately answer.

Sarah leaned back in her chair, his question echoing in her mind. This wasn't the first time she'd sensed something beneath the surface. Just weeks earlier, two high-potential managers had quietly resigned. There were no angry complaints. No talk of pay. One had simply said in her exit interview, 'I just can't see myself here anymore.'

Sarah felt a sudden jolt within her, not anger or blame, but a sinking recognition that something important had gone unnoticed. If two of her most promising leaders no longer saw a future here, how many others were already halfway out the door? And here it was again: not dissatisfaction, but disconnection. A sense of emotional drift, as Baumeister (1991) might describe it – the subtle but powerful loss of meaning that often precedes burnout, attrition or 'quiet quitting' (Gallup, 2023).

Sarah's mind scanned the data. Revenue was up. Engagement survey scores were stable. Attrition was at benchmark. But none of those metrics captured what had just happened in the room – the sudden honesty. A deeper pattern was forming – one that the dashboards didn't register. 'Let's not pretend everything is fine,' she said firmly. 'I want us to come back to this.'

What Sarah was noticing – without yet naming it – was the Purpose-to-Meaning Gap. It wasn't that people didn't understand the company's purpose. It was that they didn't feel connected to it. The mission was clear, but the meaning wasn't landing. The company said, *Shape the future.* Her people were asking, *What does that mean for me today?*

This is what Gallup (2023) warns about: the rise of disengagement not as rebellion, but quiet retreat – the emotional cost of meaning that never quite materializes. People still show up. But the spark is gone. And eventually, so are they.

Sarah remained seated as the others filed out. Her hand still gripped the pen. Tariq's words had struck like a small earthquake, revealing cracks in assumptions she hadn't thought to question. NexusNova's purpose was printed on the wall just outside the boardroom. But if it wasn't being felt in the lived experience of work, what difference did it make?

And if someone as engaged as Tariq felt it, she suspected many others did too.

Sarah's experience wasn't the exception. It reflected a deeper, more systemic pattern, that's quietly shaping workplaces across all industries. Next, let's explore what drives that disconnection and how leaders can begin to close the meaning gap between strategy and felt experience.

Defining the gap: an emergency coaching session

That evening, Sarah found herself pacing the floor of her mid-week stay London apartment, a short ten minute walk from their head office. She replayed Tariq's words and the uncomfortable silence that had followed. NexusNova's purpose statement – *Powering the platforms that shape the future and help every person thrive* – had once been her pride. It had launched with fanfare: sleek marketing, an all-hands town hall, strategic comms campaigns. It was clear. Ambitious. Inspiring.

And yet… it now felt oddly hollow.

She sighed, opened her laptop and scrolled through the latest dashboards again. Everything looked fine. Engagement survey scores were up two points. Voluntary attrition was trending below industry average. But none of it explained what she'd just witnessed. No metric had warned her of the truth voiced by Tariq – or the truth behind the quiet resignations. Sarah was starting to suspect that her organization had a problem with measurement. They were missing something deeper.

She remembered the Gallup headline, that only 21% of employees globally are thriving, the rest disengaged or going through the motions. Was NexusNova any different? Or were the numbers just showing the cracks in the foundations? What she was seeing was not a failure of purpose but a breakdown in how purpose was felt: early signs of the Purpose-to-Meaning Gap.

Admitting she needed help, Sarah typed a quick email to her longtime executive coach: *Angela – can we speak first thing tomorrow? Something important's come up.*

Early next morning, Sarah arrived at Angela's office in Marleybone. The sun was barely up, but the space was warm, calm and inviting – a welcome contrast to the emotional noise in her head. After settling into the armchair, she began talking: the meeting, Tariq's honesty, the uneasy silence, the familiar data points that had told her... nothing.

Angela listened without interruption; pen poised over a notebook. When Sarah finally paused, Angela leaned forward slightly.

'You're not describing a typical engagement problem,' she said. 'What you're describing is something we call a meaning gap.' *(See Appendix 1 for a practical diagnostic to uncover where this may be present in your teams.)*

Sarah was puzzled. 'Is that like the purpose gap people talk about?' she asked.

Angela nodded gently. 'It's related,' she said. 'A purpose gap is when your company's purpose isn't translating into its employees' daily experiences. A meaning gap is when employees no longer feel emotionally connected to their work, even if they understand the purpose. The gap between what the company says and what people feel – that's the Purpose-to-Meaning Gap.'

She paused, letting that sink in. 'In other words, purpose lives in the boardroom, but meaning lives in the hearts of employees' (Bloom, 2018).

Her words landed. Sarah sat back in her chair. She'd been so focused on communicating purpose – the big *why* – that she'd overlooked what people were actually experiencing every day.

Angela continued. 'Think of Kahn's research on engagement,' she said. 'He found that people only engage fully when work feels psychologically meaningful – when they feel valued, aligned and seen in their role' (Kahn, 1990). 'Without that, even great strategy starts to feel... abstract.'

Sarah nodded slowly. 'So, even if the mission is bold, people can still feel adrift.'

'Exactly. They might agree with the purpose – but not see themselves in it.'

Sarah thought about the tools she'd relied on. Gallup's Q12 surveys; engagement dashboards; focus group summaries; questions designed to track morale and motivation. But had any of them ever asked: *Does your work feel meaningful?*

Sarah's eyes widened with a new insight. 'We've been measuring the output – engagement,' she said slowly, 'but not the input – meaning.'

'That's exactly the shift we need,' Angela replied. 'If you want to manage something as vital as culture, you must measure it. Right now, we're missing the ingredients of engagement – the things that make work feel meaningful. Think about it: factors like alignment with one's values and purpose, opportunities for growth, genuine connection with others and a sense of resonance or personal fulfilment. Those are the core elements that drive meaning at work. And those,' she added, 'are what I'd call your Meaning Metrics.'

Sarah nodded, the idea clicking into place. She realized these concepts weren't entirely new. Psychologists and leadership experts had long identified similar drivers – for instance, Pink (2011) had highlighted intrinsic motivators like autonomy, mastery and purpose. These ingredients of meaningful work had been discussed in leadership circles and even in some of her own mentoring sessions with emerging leaders. The difference now was seeing them as measurable. Angela was reframing soft ideas into something concrete: not just motivational levers, but measurable indicators of cultural health.

Angela pointed to her notebook, where she had jotted a few data points. 'Gallup's 2022 report showed that engagement alone can be misleading,' she noted. 'People can score high on things like workplace friendships or recognition yet still feel hollow in their contribution' (Gallup, 2022). She looked back at Sarah. 'In other words, you can have decent surface-level engagement for a while – but if those deeper meaning drivers are missing, the energy and enthusiasm won't last. Especially during times of stress or change.'

Sarah recalled research by Luthans, Youssef and Avolio (2007) on Psychological Capital – how hope, efficacy, resilience and optimism all rise when work feels purposeful. Meaning wasn't just emotional fluff; it was fuel.

'And that's when you start seeing disengagement,' Angela said. 'People don't quit overnight. First, they quietly quit – pulling back their effort, disengaging emotionally' (Gallup, 2023). 'And eventually, they leave.'

Sarah thought again of the two managers who had left with grace and no complaints. No red flags, just a shared, unspoken truth: *This work doesn't mean enough to me anymore.*

Angela reached into her folder and passed Sarah a printout from a McKinsey report on workplace meaning.

'Here,' she said, 'is why this matters.'

Sarah scanned the page:

- Employees who find their work meaningful are 33% more productive
- They are 75% more committed
- They are 49% less likely to leave (McKinsey, 2021)

'This is the business case,' Angela said. 'Meaning drives outcomes. When it's missing, all the engagement programmes in the world won't stick.'

Sarah nodded. She'd always thought of purpose as the answer. But now, she was starting to see that meaning was the missing link – the part that had never been fully translated into the day-to-day.

Her people weren't rejecting the mission. They were searching for a sense of personal connection to it.

That, she now realized, was her new job: to close the Purpose-to-Meaning Gap, not through words, but through leadership.

Case in action – Microsoft's meaningful work transformation

Angela flipped to the final page of the printout she'd brought.

'Take a look at this example,' she said.

The title read: *Case in action – Microsoft's meaningful work transformation.*

As Sarah read, the pieces began to fall into place. Under CEO Satya Nadella's leadership, Microsoft had undergone more than a technological evolution – it had rebuilt its culture from the inside out. The shift wasn't driven by a new product or strategy alone. It was fuelled by a radical refocus on meaning.

Nadella had moved the company from a know-it-all, siloed environment to a learn-it-all, human-centred one. His leadership championed growth mindset, personal development, emotional intelligence and inclusion. And critically, he had helped employees connect what they did every day to something that mattered.

Microsoft's internal data showed the results: employee engagement improved, collaboration increased, innovation accelerated. The company's market value skyrocketed from around $300 billion to nearly $3 trillion (The Economic Times, 2024).

'It's not just culture for culture's sake,' Angela said. 'They translated purpose into meaning. And it paid off.'

Sarah nodded. The results were undeniable. But what struck her even more was how Nadella had achieved it – by making meaning personal. The transformation wasn't top-down or symbolic. It was lived. Measured. Felt.

Angela pointed to another line in the report:

'Microsoft linked daily tasks to personal growth and connected roles to the company's mission. That's how they made meaning real – not just inspirational' (Microsoft Research, 2022).

Sarah looked up. 'So, it's not about adding meaning on top of the work. It's about designing meaning into the work.'

Angela smiled. 'Exactly. The companies that thrive don't treat meaningful work as a bonus – they treat it as a system.'

Sarah's eyes returned to the final paragraph. A quote was highlighted:

> *'Purpose, when lived through daily behaviour and systems, becomes felt meaning. That's where culture changes – and performance follows.'*
> *(McKinsey and Company, 2021)*

She sat back. A quiet conviction settling in.

'So, we don't just need to communicate our purpose better,' she said slowly. 'We need to operationalize it. Translate it. Help people feel it in their actual work.'

Angela nodded. 'That's how you close the Purpose-to-Meaning Gap – not through a speech, but through culture, leadership and systems.'

Sarah exhaled deeply. For the first time since the meeting with Tariq, she didn't just feel concerned – she felt clear. There was a way forward. A strategy she could develop. And a shift that would matter far beyond retention numbers.

Because this wasn't just about performance. This was about creating a company she would still want to work for.

Bridging the gap – the framework and Sarah's turning point

Angela stood and moved to the whiteboard. She picked up a marker and drew two columns. On the left, she wrote:

PURPOSE

Vision. Mission. Strategy.

On the right:

MEANING

Fulfilment. Connection. Personal Values.

Between them, she sketched a wide chasm.

'This is the Purpose-to-Meaning Gap,' she said. 'It's the space between what the organization says and what people feel.' *(See Figure 1)*

She wrote three words in the middle of the gap, underlining each in red:

Burnout. Disengagement. Attrition.

'When this gap is left unaddressed,' she continued, 'these are the outcomes that fall into it.'

Sarah stared at the board. The visual struck a nerve. The left side – their strategy, purpose, performance metrics – was well-polished. The right side – the employee experience – was where the cracks had formed.

'So, this is what we've been missing,' she said. 'Not the strategy. Not the purpose. But the translation into felt meaning.'

Angela nodded. 'Employees today expect more than a clear mission. They expect a personal connection to that mission. That's the shift.' Research shows that employees are no longer satisfied with pay and job titles alone. They want growth, alignment, impact – and they want to feel it in the work they do every day (Gallup, 2023).

Sarah recalled the recent resignations. The subtle disengagement in meetings. Tariq's question. It all mapped to this diagram.

Angela stepped back.

'The only way to close this gap,' she said, 'is through leadership, culture and systems – not one big initiative, but a set of daily, human actions that embed meaning into how the organization runs.'

Sarah nodded slowly. 'So, it's not about having a better speech at the next town hall. It's about how we design the experience of work.'

'Exactly,' Angela replied. 'This is why the Meaning Over Purpose blueprint exists. It helps leaders operationalize meaningful work – at scale.'

Sarah sat back in her chair. The quiet urgency she'd felt after the leadership meeting had now transformed into a sense of resolve. She knew what needed to happen next.

They mapped out a plan – confidential listening sessions to better understand what meaning *meant* to different employee groups, an audit of existing people practices through the lens of fulfilment and alignment, and a new leadership narrative that put meaning at the centre of their culture strategy.

'I need to bring this to the full executive team,' Sarah said. 'And we need to lead this together.'

Angela smiled. 'That's what great leaders do. They don't just write the mission – they make it *matter*.'

Final Reflection

That evening, back in her home office, Sarah picked up the phone and called Tariq.

'Thank you for what you said yesterday,' she told him. 'You helped open a conversation that we needed to have. And I'd value your input as we move forward.'

Tariq's surprise was audible. 'Thank you, Sarah. I'm here to help however I can.'

After the call, Sarah stood by the window and looked out over the city. She realized that real leadership – the kind that builds cultures people want to be part of – didn't begin with a plan. It began with listening. With questions. With courage.

And with meaning.

'This is the work worth doing,' she thought.

And for the first time in a long while, she felt truly ready to lead differently.

Takeaways

- When meaning is embedded organizations see stronger loyalty, greater innovation, lower burnout and more sustainable performance. These are not soft outcomes – they're business-critical.

- Meaningful work drives results: higher employee commitment, innovation and lower turnover come from meaningful daily experiences, not just well-crafted purpose statements. The business case is real. For example, employees who find their work meaningful are 33% more productive, 75% more committed and 49% less likely to leave (McKinsey and Company, 2021).

- Purpose gap vs. meaning gap: a purpose gap is the misalignment between a company's stated purpose and employees' reality. A meaning gap is more personal – a lack of fulfilment in the role itself. Both gaps undermine engagement if left unaddressed (Bloom, 2018; Kahn, 1990).

- Listen beyond the metrics: traditional engagement surveys and dashboards may not flag a meaning gap. Employees often disengage quietly, not through complaints but through emotional withdrawal, what Gallup (2023) describes as 'quiet quitting.' Leaders must look beyond surface metrics and explore meaning as an input to performance (Gallup, 2022; Luthans, Youssef and Avolio, 2007).

Reflection Questions

1. When was the last time you asked your people what meaning they get from their work? What did you learn?

2. How closely does your organization's lofty mission align with employees' day-to-day experiences? What's one practical step you can take now to bridge any gaps?

3. Are you prepared to treat meaningful work as a strategic imperative? What will you do in the next 90 days to start shifting your culture from purpose-driven to meaning-driven?

Chapter 2
From purpose to meaning – the new leadership imperative

> 'Leadership is not about being in charge. It is about
> taking care of those in your charge.'
> Simon Sinek

Summary

Here we explore why purpose is no longer enough. In today's disrupted landscape, leaders are under pressure to respond to accelerating change, shifting employee expectations and a growing wellbeing crisis. Sarah McKinnon, CEO of NexusNova, begins to see that despite articulating a compelling purpose, her organization is not immune to disconnection and disengagement.

Through Sarah's experiences and the lens of four converging megatrends – automation and AI, generational value shifts, rising burnout and hybrid work – we examine the growing imperative for leaders to move beyond purpose and create meaningful work experiences that are personal, resonant and lasting.

Research from Deloitte (2021) and PwC (2022) reveals that younger generations increasingly seek alignment with personal values, flexibility and fulfilment – not just purpose on paper. Gallup (2023) highlights the rise of 'quiet quitting' as a symptom of deeper disengagement, particularly in hybrid environments (Gallup, 2023; IBM, 2021). Burnout is now recognized by the World Health Organization as an occupational phenomenon, exacerbated by poor workplace connection and lack of perceived impact (WHO, 2019; Maslach and Leiter, 2016). It is an enduring issue, with 48% of workers and 53% of managers reporting experiencing burnout at work (Deloitte, 2024).

Sarah begins to understand that her challenge isn't simply about clarifying strategy or refining communication – it's about helping people make sense of their work. This chapter establishes why embedding meaning is the next leadership frontier – a human response to a system in flux.

The Future of Work summit – setting the stage for disruption

The hotel ballroom buzzed with polite urgency – all suits, swivel badges and elegantly frothed flat whites.

Sarah scanned the room as she took her seat near the front. She'd flown into Berlin that morning for the Future of Work summit, an annual gathering of senior leaders, economists and futurists convened to discuss trends shaping the next decade. It was her third time attending – and one of the few events she still prioritized. The theme this year was *Human-First, Tech-Fast: Reimagining Work in a Disrupted World.*

Just before the session began, Sarah spotted a familiar figure a few rows ahead – Giovanni Mancini, CEO of LyriaTech. She hadn't seen him in person since the industry awards the previous year. As always, he was impeccably dressed, already chatting animatedly with another CEO.

Giovanni had been a force in the sector for two decades – confident, data-driven, relentlessly strategic. Sarah respected his track record. But she also remembered how, in past conversations, he'd often rolled his eyes at phrases like 'culture journey' or 'human-first leadership'.

'Engagement's nice,' he'd once said to her. 'But performance is what matters.'

The moderator, a futurist from an AI think tank, opened the summit with a stat from the World Economic Forum Future of Jobs Report (2025):

'In the next five years, structural labour market changes will affect 22% of jobs, with approximately 170 million new jobs created. With over half of employers planning to reorient their business around AI, this means over one billion people will need to reskill as AI and automation reshape global industries.'

Heads nodded. No one in the room was surprised.

Giovanni was among the first to speak on the CEO panel that followed.

'We've invested heavily in AI and are already seeing double-digit efficiency gains,' he said. 'Our focus now is on building technical agility and making sure we retain people who can think fast and adapt.'

The comment was met with applause. Sarah clapped too, but slowly. She knew Giovanni's business was thriving. But she also wondered what the human cost of speed was becoming.

Another panellist cited PwC's (2022) *Hopes and Fears* survey, noting that 59% of global employees were rethinking the role work played in their lives, requiring a new psychological contract between organizations and the people working for them. A third panellist added a stat from Deloitte's 2024 *Gen Z and Millennial* survey: '44% of Gen Zs and 40% of Millennials have declined job offers from employers whose values didn't align with their own.'

'We're seeing culture become the biggest recruitment and retention lever,' they said.

Giovanni's response was measured.

'Culture's important – but at the end of the day, what retains people is opportunity. Purpose is a bonus. Let's not get distracted.'

There it was. Sarah scribbled a note.

'Opportunity without meaning = churn.'

As Sarah wrote those words, she thought back to Jasmin, a brilliant young data scientist who led a sprint the previous month. Her work was exceptional – but what stayed with Sarah wasn't just the output. It was a comment that Jasmin had made during a reverse mentoring session: 'I need to feel like the work we're doing actually matters every day and has a positive impact on the world.' It was no longer enough to offer opportunity; her generation expected meaning.

The moderator pivoted to a discussion on hybrid work. Analysts from IBM (2021) and Gartner (2022a) shared data on rising disconnection, cultural drift and the risk of emotional disengagement in flexible models.

Sarah wrote a note in her notebook to reflect on later:

'We've become efficient. But have we stayed connected?'

As the panel wrapped up, Giovanni shared one last prediction.

'The next decade will belong to leaders who can digitize faster than their competitors.'

Sarah wasn't so sure anymore.

'Or maybe,' she thought, 'it will belong to leaders who can humanize faster.' And this would need to be a CEO-led imperative. That quiet instinct would follow her into the next chapter of her leadership.

To understand why meaning is now the leadership mandate, we must first examine how the very deal between employer and employee has evolved. This isn't philosophical, it is strategic. What Sarah is sensing and what the research now confirms is that purpose alone can't meet the emotional contract of modern work.

Let's explore why meaning is now a leadership imperative.

The future is changing faster than we are

Sarah closed the lid of her laptop and exhaled slowly. Her virtual executive meeting had wrapped up ten minutes ago, but she hadn't moved. Something about the call had unsettled her but she couldn't quite name what.

The team had walked through their standard updates: customer growth in Asia Pacific, AI acceleration in product development, the new diversity strategy in EMEA. The conversations were competent. The slides were polished. But the energy was… flat. Her eye drifted to the purpose statement printed on the card next to her monitor:

Powering the platforms that shape the future and help every person thrive.

She'd signed off on it last year, proud of the language, the vision, the clarity. But something in her gut told her it wasn't enough anymore. The team had nodded, but they hadn't lit up. No questions. No challenge. No spark.

She sat back and muttered to herself:

'The world has moved on – but have we?'

Global forces were converging, faster than ever. The World Economic Forum had warned that by 2025, automation and AI would displace up to 85 million jobs – but also create 97 million new ones (World Economic Forum, 2020). That meant millions of people would need to retrain, reorient and reimagine their role in the world of work.

It wasn't just AI. Sarah was seeing it in the generational dynamics too. She recalled the summit stat from Deloitte's (2021) *Millennial and Gen Z* survey that had been sobering: over 60% of younger workers said they would leave their current employer if their values didn't align. More than half ranked wellbeing and personal impact as more important than promotion or pay. PwC's (2022) global survey backed it up: employees were reassessing not just where they work, but *why* they work.

These were not temporary trends. They were signals of a deeper shift: people were demanding more from work – not in perks, but in purpose, connection and personal meaning.

And then there was burnout.

Sarah had spent years brushing off low energy as part of the job. But now, it was everywhere. Even her most committed leaders seemed depleted. The World Health Organization had formally classified burnout as an occupational phenomenon in 2019 – caused by unmanaged workplace stress, not personal weakness (WHO, 2019). And as Maslach and Leiter (2016) explained, burnout was often the result of a mismatch between people and their work – especially in values, autonomy, reward or community.

'Burnout isn't just about workload,' Angela had told her in a recent coaching session. 'It's about meaning erosion.'

That phrase stuck with her.

Sarah stood and looked around her home office. Since the pandemic, she'd become used to leading from behind a screen. But she was increasingly aware of what was missing. The hallway conversations. The impromptu laughter after a client win. The spontaneous brainstorming over lunch. Digital tools were efficient but they didn't make people feel seen.

She wasn't alone in thinking this. Research from IBM (2021) found that hybrid work, while offering flexibility, could weaken employee connection and engagement if not designed thoughtfully. Gartner's (2022b) study showed that nearly 60% of hybrid employees felt less connected to their organization's mission than they did pre-pandemic.

Sarah looked back down at the purpose statement on her desk. It hadn't changed but the context around it had, and so had the people. Unless she led differently, she knew the next chapter of NexusNova's growth story wouldn't be shaped by technology or talent. It would be shaped by meaning – or the lack of it.

Angela's words echoed from their last coaching session – but this time, Sarah heard them differently.

'These aren't just market forces,' Angela had said.

'They're accelerants. Each one widens the Purpose-to-Meaning Gap in a different way. And together, they form the perfect storm that leaders must now navigate.'

Sarah had spent weeks tracking patterns – from boardroom conversations to frontline feedback, from the perspectives of senior and middle managers, from exit interviews to coaching reflections. One thing had become clear: these were not isolated challenges. They were converging pressures reshaping not just how people work, but how they feel about work.

Each force, she realized, wasn't simply a disruption to react to. It was a design challenge. A leadership opportunity. A moment to close the gap – or widen it.

She pulled out her notebook and underlined some words in bold:

AI and automation → identity redesign

More than efficiency gains, this was about value. As tasks get automated, people ask: *What's left for me?* Leaders must help redefine roles around contribution, not task repetition.

Generational shifts → value recalibration

Millennials and Gen Z are not just asking for flexibility – they're asking for alignment. They expect authenticity, meaning and growth. Culture is no longer a 'nice-to-have'; it's the deal.

Burnout → energy strategy

Exhaustion is everywhere – not from effort alone, but from misalignment. People aren't just tired. They're disconnected. Meaning isn't a perk here – it's fuel. And it must be designed into the system.

Hybrid culture → belonging by design

Flexible work has delivered convenience, but not always connection. The informal bonds are thinning. Rituals are vanishing. Belonging must be built intentionally or it fades.

The four forces reshaping leadership
Why the future demands a shift to meaning

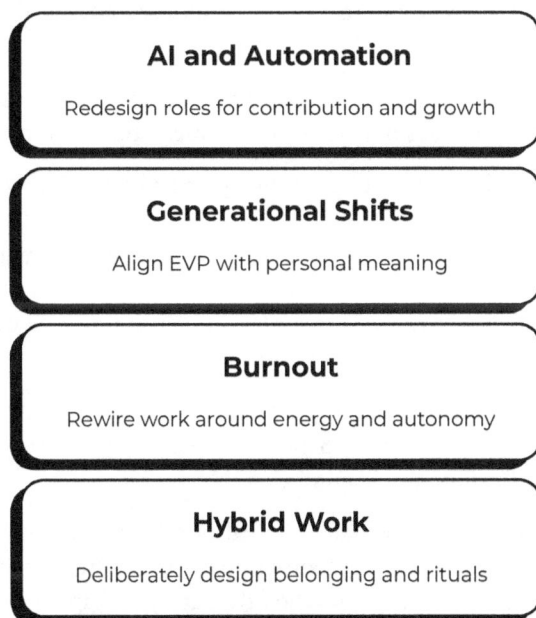

AI and Automation

Redesign roles for contribution and growth

Generational Shifts

Align EVP with personal meaning

Burnout

Rewire work around energy and autonomy

Hybrid Work

Deliberately design belonging and rituals

Figure 4: Each of these forces is reshaping not just how we work, but how we feel about work. Left unchecked, they widen the Purpose-to-Meaning Gap. But when leaders respond with intention, these forces become catalysts for deeper alignment, connection and performance.

Sarah sat back, her pen resting on the page. These weren't surface challenges; they were deep shifts in the emotional contract of work. If leaders failed to respond, the Purpose-to-Meaning Gap would only grow wider.

But if they did respond? Each force could become a catalyst, not just for adaptation but for reinvention.

The four forces reshaping the meaning landscape

Later that week, Sarah walked slowly through NexusNova's London headquarters, her eyes scanning the light-filled spaces that once buzzed with energy which now seemed the exception rather than the rule. On some days, whole departments worked remotely. On others, a handful of people floated through, headphones on, cameras off.

She paused by the café. Once the unofficial heart of the business – a hub for cross-functional conversations and informal collaboration – it now sat mostly quiet. The espresso machine still steamed, but the laughter was gone.

'The rituals have changed,' she thought, 'and so has the connection. We've kept the meetings but we've lost the meaningful moments.'

She wasn't imagining it. Gallup's 2023 report had given it a name: 'quiet quitting.' Employees were doing their jobs but pulling back their energy, their spark. The emotional contract was fraying in hybrid environments. Sarah knew they would never return fully to the office, full time, so she needed to understand the factors at play and reimagine how work could be better for people in this new world.

Angela's voice came back to her from their last conversation: 'There are four forces at play right now, Sarah. And every single one of them is widening the Purpose-to-Meaning Gap.'

Sarah sat down at a corner table, pulled out her notebook and began writing down what she'd been observing – the patterns that weren't showing up on performance dashboards, but were shaping how people showed up at work.

1. AI and automation are creating an identity crisis

AI was no longer a future threat – it was already transforming how NexusNova operated. From content generation to predictive analytics, automation had started replacing repetitive tasks at scale. On paper, this was a win: cost savings, speed, efficiency. But Sarah had also seen the other side. Good people, especially in operations, customer support and HR, were quietly wondering if their roles still mattered.

'If a system can do my job,' one mid-level manager had said during a coaching session, 'where does that leave me?'

The World Economic Forum predicted this displacement and creation dynamic – millions of roles would vanish and new ones would emerge. But the real challenge wasn't job loss. It was meaning loss. As more roles became augmented or automated, employees were struggling to see where they fitted in, in a world where over half of all employers are reshaping their businesses with AI (WEF, 2024). They weren't asking, *Am I valuable?* They were asking, *Am I still necessary?*

2. New generations, new expectations

Sarah thought of Maya, a 27-year-old UX designer who had recently led a product sprint with outstanding results. Her work had been brilliant but what stood out more was what she said to her line manager during her development review: 'I need to feel like the work we're doing actually matters. Otherwise, I'll find somewhere else that does.'

When this was shared with her in the talent review session, Sarah had nodded, taken a note and later circled it twice.

Maya's mindset wasn't unusual, and reinforced Sarah's previous conversation with Jasmin. Deloitte's (2021) *Gen Z and Millennial* survey showed that younger workers are increasingly unwilling to compromise on alignment in their desire for purpose-driven careers. PwC (2022) found similar results. Employees under 35 years of age were the most likely to switch jobs in search of meaning and cultural fit – not salary.

Sarah thought back to her early career. Back then, purpose was a bonus. Today, it was a baseline.

3. Burnout is no longer a private struggle

Just last month, Sarah had spoken with Jamal – a brilliant strategy director who'd recently taken two weeks of unplanned leave. He hadn't complained. He hadn't demanded anything. He'd just said, 'I feel completely depleted.'

Jamal wasn't the only one.

The World Health Organization (2019) had formally recognized burnout as a workplace condition – not a personal failing. Maslach and Leiter (2016) had long warned that burnout wasn't just about long hours or workload. It was about emotional misalignment – when people no longer felt connected to what they were doing or who they were doing it for.

Sarah wrote in her notebook: *Exhaustion isn't just about energy. It's about purposelessness.* She wondered how many others were feeling the same but were just quieter about it.

4. Hybrid work has disrupted connection and culture

NexusNova had embraced hybrid work early. Productivity hadn't dropped. In fact, some teams reported working 'smarter.' But something else had slipped. The glue between people. The informal bonds that made people stay a little longer after meetings. The sense of shared purpose that didn't need to be spoken – it was just *felt*.

Gartner reported that nearly 60% of hybrid employees feel less connected to their company's mission in 2022, and 41% of HR leaders in 2024 echoed that this connection to culture is being compromised (Gartner, 2022c; 2024). IBM (2021) had highlighted that even high performers were at risk of detachment without deliberate cultural interventions.

Sarah had seen this first-hand. It wasn't about remote versus office. It was about the quality of connection – emotional, not just logistical.

She leaned back in her chair, absorbing the list:

- AI
- Generational expectations
- Burnout
- Hybrid culture

Each was real. Each was reshaping how people experienced work. And together, they were driving the single greatest leadership challenge she had faced yet: not just articulating purpose but activating meaning.

The leadership wake-up call

Later that evening, Sarah sat in her home office with a cup of tea, flipping back through her notes. The phrase Angela had used in their last session kept echoing in her mind: *This isn't a talent issue. It's a meaning issue.*

The words felt sharper now. She looked again at the four forces she'd listed – AI, generational values, burnout, hybrid – and saw something she hadn't before.

They weren't just background conditions. They were pressure points – each one stretching the gap between what the company said it stood for and how people actually experienced their work.

She opened her laptop and pulled up the latest engagement dashboard. Numbers were holding. Attrition hadn't spiked. Feedback was… fine.

But now she knew better. Fine was a red flag. Gallup (2022) had shown that employees often report stable engagement scores even as they begin emotionally disconnecting – because the metrics track *conditions*, not *connection*. It wasn't that the surveys were flawed. It was that they were incomplete. And the gap between surface engagement and inner meaning was growing.

Sarah's cursor hovered over the company's updated purpose statement, that had just been approved by the board, in the internal comms deck:

> *We exist to empower every human to thrive in a digitally connected world.*

She read it aloud. Then again.

It was clear. It was inspiring.

But was it felt?

Angela had been right: many organizations articulate purpose from the top – but fail to translate it into the daily reality of the people doing the work. The result? Employees hear the company's *why*, but struggle to connect it to their own *why me?*

This was the Purpose-to-Meaning Gap in action. And Sarah now saw it not just as a cultural risk but as a strategic blind spot.

Research from McKinsey (2021) found that employees who see their work as meaningful are not only more engaged, but also more productive (+33%), more committed (+75%) and significantly less likely to leave (+49%). The return on meaning wasn't theoretical. It was measurable.

She scribbled a note in her notebook: *Meaning isn't just emotional – it's operational.*

Angela had framed it clearly during one of their strategy sessions: 'The future will belong to organizations that embed meaning into how they lead, not just into what they say.'

Sarah paused. She looked again at her screen, then out the window.

The skyline hadn't changed. But she had.

From strategy to daily experience

The next morning, Sarah arrived early at NexusNova's leadership offsite in Lisbon. The agenda had been cleared for a single topic: the cultural reset.

The room buzzed softly as her direct reports arrived. Coffee. Post-it® notes. Laptops open. On the surface, it felt like any other leadership day. But this time, Sarah knew the conversation needed to go deeper.

She opened the session with honesty.

'We've done a lot of work on purpose over the past year. But I want us to ask a different question today: What does that purpose actually feel like to our people – in their real, everyday work?'

There was a pause. Then Leonie spoke first.

'Honestly? I think for a lot of people, it feels... distant. They know the words. They just don't know what it has to do with their day-to-day.'

Several heads nodded. Tariq added, 'We're good at cascading strategy. We're not as good at making it mean something.'

Sarah had been waiting for that. She stepped to the front of the room and sketched a version of Angela's whiteboard visual: 'Purpose' on one side, 'Meaning' on the other, a gap in between.

'We've got a strong purpose,' she said. 'But if it doesn't connect to personal values, relationships or contribution, it doesn't land. People need to feel their work matters. Every day. Otherwise, it's just noise.'

The team broke into smaller groups, each tasked with answering a simple question: *Where are we accidentally making work meaningless?*

The answers came quickly:

- Project metrics with no feedback loop
- Quarterly reviews that focused only on delivery, not development
- Recognition tied to performance, but never to impact
- New joiners overwhelmed by systems before they meet their teams
- Hybrid days with no deliberate rituals to build belonging

As the lists grew, Sarah could see it clearly. The challenge wasn't a lack of intent – it was a lack of integration. Meaning wasn't showing up in the systems, the behaviours or the conversations that defined people's experience of work.

'This is it,' she thought. 'This is where we close the gap.'

Later that day, she shared a framework Angela had introduced – the one she now saw as a compass: meaning must be felt through Autonomy, Mastery, Purpose, Connection and Impact. Together, these pillars helped diagnose not just whether people were engaged, but why – or why not (Pink, 2011; Grant, 2013; Luthans, Youssef and Avolio, 2007).

'We've measured engagement for years,' she told the group. 'Now we need to measure meaning. We need to design for it. Embed it. Model it.'

Heads nodded again but this time it was different. The room felt less like a strategy session and more like a turning point.

Sarah closed the day with a simple challenge.

'Next quarter, let's make this real. Let's choose five moments that matter – and redesign them to activate meaning.'

Not a programme. Not a campaign.

A shift: from purpose written on the wall to meaning experienced at work.

Meaning as the new leadership advantage

As the offsite wrapped, Sarah lingered at the back of the room, watching her executive team gather their notes and close their laptops. Something had shifted – not just in the discussion, but in the atmosphere.

It wasn't enthusiasm. Not yet. It was clarity.

She knew this wasn't a one-off moment. It was the start of something deeper. A change in how they would lead, measure and talk about culture, not just through dashboards but through meaning.

On the flight home that evening, she jotted down a single question in her notebook: *What if meaning isn't just a retention strategy – but a competitive advantage?*

It was more than rhetorical. She'd seen the data: companies that embed meaning systemically see not only higher employee engagement, but greater innovation, customer satisfaction and long-term growth (McKinsey and Company, 2021). Research from Gallup (2023) showed that teams who feel their work is meaningful outperform peers on key metrics like productivity, profitability and quality.

The reason? Meaning fuels discretionary effort – the kind of above-and-beyond energy that no incentive scheme can buy.

But there was something even more powerful at play.

Meaning created resilience. Studies on psychological capital – the internal resources of hope, confidence and optimism – show that employees who find meaning in their work are significantly more adaptable, creative and motivated under pressure (Luthans, Youssef and Avolio, 2007). In times of disruption, they don't just cope – they contribute.

'Meaning makes people stay,' Sarah thought. 'But more than that – it helps them lead.'

She gazed out the window with a deepening clarity and conviction of the task ahead. Her perspective had changed. The leadership challenge wasn't to continually rewrite the purpose to make it more compelling; it was to bring it to life – through moments, systems and behaviours that allowed every person to feel it.

This wasn't about purpose instead *of* performance.

It was about performance through meaning.

And that, she knew now, was the new leadership imperative.

Final Reflection

Later that night, Sarah scrolled through the summit feed on LinkedIn. Photos of the event were already circulating – polished panels, branded stages, applause. Her own keynote quote was trending modestly.

'The future of work will be human or it won't work at all.'

She stared at the screen.

It wasn't wrong. But it wasn't complete either.

She thought about the offsite. The silence on the Zoom call. Jamal's burnout. Jasmin and Maya's honest feedback. The meaningful moments that never made it into slide decks but defined whether people stayed, showed up fully or slowly drifted away.

She was starting to see it clearly now: purpose was what they had; meaning was what they were missing. And it wouldn't be solved by adding another initiative. It would take a different kind of leadership: quieter, braver, closer. The kind of leadership that doesn't just declare the *why* but helps people feel their own reason to care.

'That,' she thought, 'is what we lead next.'

Takeaways

- **Purpose is not enough.** Today's workforce – especially younger generations – expects more than an inspiring statement. They want to feel that their work matters, every day. Deloitte (2021) and PwC (2022) found that alignment with values, wellbeing and personal impact now outweigh traditional markers of success like pay and promotion.

- The four forces are accelerants of the Purpose-to-Meaning Gap. AI disruption, generational value shifts, burnout and hybrid work are not isolated challenges – they are converging megatrends reshaping the emotional contract of work. Left unaddressed, each one widens the Purpose-to-Meaning Gap. But when treated as design challenges, each becomes a leadership opportunity for reinvention and resonance.

- Meaning must be embedded, not just announced. Leaders often assume that articulating purpose is enough – but if people can't feel it in their roles, systems and interactions, it won't land. Gallup (2022) warns that organizations risk misreading steady engagement scores if they're not measuring the underlying drivers of meaning.

- Meaning drives performance and resilience. Research from McKinsey (2021) and Gallup (2023) shows that employees who find their work meaningful are more productive, committed and innovative. Luthans et al. (2007) confirm that meaning strengthens psychological capital, giving people the internal resources to thrive, not just survive, through uncertainty.

- The new leadership imperative is translation, not communication. The role of the leader is not just to set direction – it is to ensure purpose becomes felt meaning. This happens through deliberate systems, rituals, conversations and behaviours. Purpose that is not translated becomes noise. Meaning that is embedded becomes culture.

Reflection Questions

1. How confident are you that your employees experience purpose as meaningful – not just understood, but felt? What signals – beyond engagement scores – are you using to assess that connection?

2. Where in your organization might meaning be unintentionally blocked or eroded – through process, measurement, leadership behaviours or systems?

3. How are your hybrid or remote employees experiencing purpose and connection? Have you adapted your leadership rituals to ensure inclusion and cohesion?

4. In the face of AI, reskilling and disruption, how are you helping people hold onto a sense of contribution, growth and impact?

5. If each force is a leadership moment, which one will you lead next? Where can you shift from strategy-on-paper to felt meaning in practice within the next 90 days?

Chapter 3
Why the old deal is dead and the new deal is meaning-driven

'People want to know they matter and they want to
be treated as people. That is the new talent contract.'
Indra Nooyi, former CEO of PepsiCo

Summary

From here, Sarah begins to confront a deeper realization: that many of
the systems, assumptions and leadership habits she grew up with are no
longer fit for the future of work. What once served as the unspoken rules
of engagement – steady pay for loyalty, command-and-control leadership,
top-down communication – now feel increasingly outdated.

The chapter contrasts the 'old deal' of employment with the emerging
'new deal' of meaningful work – one that centres partnership, autonomy,
purpose and personal growth. Sarah realizes that her company has

made surface-level progress but still relies on legacy thinking in how it structures work, performance and leadership.

Sarah and Leonie explore how the employer–employee psychological contract is shifting (Rousseau, 1995) and how new generations are redefining what they expect from work – not just what they're paid to do, but how they're treated and what they're growing into (Deal and Levenson, 2016; SHRM, 2022). Indra Nooyi's reflections on the evolving talent contract reinforce the urgency for CEOs to move beyond lip service and redesign the experience of work itself (Nooyi, 2021).

Sarah, with Leonie's support, starts to sketch a new blueprint – one where trust, development and human connection aren't the afterthoughts of strategy, but the foundation of it.

The old deal never really left

It started with an email.

Sarah and Leonie had been reviewing performance calibration data – the quarterly process where senior managers rated team members across a five-point scale. As she read through the commentary, Sarah noticed a familiar thread: words like 'solid contributor', 'low visibility', 'follows direction well', 'independent but needs reassurance'.

None of it was malicious. In fact, the tone was supportive. But something about it felt 'off'. The language was clinical, observational and quietly rooted in a world view she now realized was out of date – one that rewarded predictability, not potential. One that valued loyalty over learning, delivery over development.

Leonie opened the performance review template and stared at the first two categories: dependability and compliance.

'We've changed our values,' Leonie thought and then shared with Sarah. 'But have we changed our lens?'

Sarah sat back in her chair and thought about what Angela had said during their last coaching session: 'The old deal is subtle. It lives in templates, behaviours, job descriptions and what you choose to reward. You can change the brand, but if you don't change the frame, people feel the gap.'

The old deal had never been formally announced – but everyone knew what it was. You showed up, followed the rules, stayed loyal and in return you got stability. Sarah thought back to her first job in finance. A steady job. A promotion pathway. A pension plan. Respect earned through tenure. She hadn't expected passion or purpose, security was enough.

It had worked for a time. Especially in large, hierarchical companies where careers spanned decades. But it was quietly collapsing. The Great Resignation made it visible. Millions of people walked away from jobs that no longer work for them.

'We don't talk about it,' Sarah wrote in her notebook. 'But we still design for it.'

She thought of Rousseau's (1995) work on psychological contracts that Leonie had shared with her a while ago – the unspoken expectations between employer and employee that shape culture far more than policies ever could. According to Rousseau, when those expectations erode – when trust is breached or loyalty goes unrewarded – disengagement follows.

And Sarah was starting to see those fractures everywhere. It wasn't that her company was hostile to growth or flexibility. In fact, the values poster on the wall proudly listed words like 'curiosity', 'collaboration' and 'courage'. But in practice? Line managers still defaulted to risk aversion. Promotions favoured those who fitted, not those who stretched. Autonomy was encouraged, but only when results were consistent.

And employees noticed. She remembered something Maya, the young designer from Chapter 2, had said during a reverse mentoring session: 'I love the company. But sometimes it feels like I'm trying to play a new game on an old board.'

Sarah had smiled at the time. But now she heard it differently.

The old deal wasn't malicious. It was inherited. And unless leaders recognized where it still lived – in systems, not just sentiments – it would quietly undermine every attempt at cultural transformation.

The old deal wasn't written down but everyone knew what it meant. Now the new work deal is emerging – one built on growth, purpose and personal alignment. Today people at work will give their all, but only if work works for them too.

Are any organizations embracing this new deal? Some forward-thinking ones are. As we saw in Chapter 1, Satya Nadella's leadership has been built on growth and psychological safety, proving that meaning-driven culture results in market-leading performance. Companies like Unilever, Patagonia and Salesforce have redesigned their employee experience to align with personal values, wellbeing and impact.

These aren't just fringe examples. They are proof that when leaders prioritize meaning, loyalty deepens, creativity returns and business results follow.

See Figure 5 for a comparison of the traditional psychological contract with today's emerging new deal – a relational model built on growth, contribution and emotional resonance.

The Old Deal	The New Deal (Meaning-Driven Work)
Job security for loyalty	Meaning for energy, growth and retention
Promotion and pay are primary motivators	Purpose, growth and impact are core motivators
Leaders deliver results	Leaders enable meaning
Culture shaped by polices and hierarchy	Culture shaped by trust, clarity and belonging
Work = tasks and productivity	Work = contribution, identity and fulfilment
Stay loyal, do more	Feel seen, grow and matter

Figure 5: The workplace contract has changed, from loyalty-for-stability to meaning-for-contribution. The old deal focused on compliance; the new deal prioritizes trust, transparency and personal growth as drivers of commitment.

What the new deal really demands

A few days later, Sarah met with Leonie to discuss feedback from the last round of exit interviews.

They pulled up the latest report, which summarized themes from employees who had left the company in the past six months. The list was short, but telling:

- Lack of growth opportunities
- Unclear path to development
- Work felt disconnected from personal goals
- Manager relationships felt transactional
- 'I wanted more than a job – I wanted something that mattered'

Sarah scanned the comments, then looked up.

'It's not the usual compensation issue,' she said. 'It's a meaning issue.'

Leonie nodded. 'They're not walking away from their roles. They're walking away from how those roles feel.'

Together, they began outlining the contours of an innovative approach. Not a replacement for performance strategy but a reframing of the leadership contract.

Sarah remembered a keynote she'd heard from Indra Nooyi several years earlier.

'The talent contract has changed. People no longer work for a pay cheque and a promotion. They work for meaning, mastery and mutual respect' (Nooyi, 2021).

That line had stuck with her – but she hadn't known what to do with it at the time.

Now it made sense.

The new deal wasn't about perks or policies. It was about how employees experienced the relationship – not just as workers, but as people.

Angela had explained it like this: 'The new deal is built on partnership. On shared accountability. On growth, not just loyalty.'

Sarah had found reinforcement for that idea in research from Hoffman, Casnocha and Yeh (2014), who described the modern employer-employee relationship not as a lifetime commitment, but as a 'tour of duty' – where both sides invest in mutual growth for a defined period. This wasn't disloyalty. It was the new loyalty – one built on honesty, impact and trust.

Similarly, SHRM (2022) had shown that leading companies were evolving their employee value proposition beyond compensation, focusing instead on meaning, flexibility, learning and purpose. Frederick (2021) argued that a growing portion of the workforce was becoming 'purpose-oriented' – people who choose jobs based on values alignment, not just pay or prestige.

Sarah reflected on how her own assumptions had shifted. When she first entered the workforce, she'd taken pride in 'toughing it out.' Long hours. Hierarchy. Patience. She respected it.

But the world was different now. And in truth, it always had been – she just hadn't questioned it.

The old deal was about performance in exchange for stability, she wrote. *The new deal is about contribution in exchange for growth.*

Naming the tension – old habits in a new era

That evening, Sarah sat alone in her home office, flipping through the workbook from a leadership retreat she'd attended the previous year. One page caught her eye:

What kind of experience do people have of being led
by you?

She remembered the session well. She'd written all the right words: clear, empowering, consistent, human.

But now, with fresh eyes, she wondered: *Had she truly lived those words?*

Her mind drifted back to her first leadership role. The model had been simple: command, deliver, impress. She'd worked hard, stayed late, managed risk tightly and rewarded those who did the same. She wasn't proud of every decision – but it had worked. At least, it used to.

She recalled something Angela had said during an earlier coaching conversation: 'Old leadership habits don't disappear when we change our values. They hide inside our rituals.'

That landed. Sarah began listing some of those rituals in her notebook:

- Weekly updates that measured deliverables, but never asked about development

- Town halls that recited values, but rarely connected them to lived examples

- 1:1s that focused on tasks, not aspirations

- Promotions that rewarded results, not reflection

- Emails signed 'Best,' when what she really wanted to say was 'Thank you'

We're trying to play the new deal, she wrote, *with old deal instruments.*

She thought of the work of Meister and Willyerd (2010), who had predicted over a decade ago that the 2020 workplace would demand radically different leadership – grounded in flexibility, feedback, collaboration and meaning. It wasn't just a generational issue. It was a structural one. Leadership was no longer about control – it was about connection.

Even the traits organizations prized were evolving. In his book *The Ideal Team Player*, Lencioni (2016) described humility, hunger and emotional intelligence as the new gold standard – not charisma, technical mastery or tenure. The same shift was showing up in internal performance data at NexusNova: the most resilient, collaborative teams weren't the ones with the most experience. They were the ones with the strongest culture of trust.

Sarah wrote a simple phrase in bold at the top of her notes:

The old deal rewards outcomes. The new deal develops people.

That was the shift.

And it had to start with her.

Rewriting the deal – building a culture of mutual growth

At the next executive team meeting, Sarah arrived with a single slide.

No metrics. No charts. Just a heading:

The New Deal at NexusNova: What We Expect and What We Offer

She looked around the room. 'We've talked about culture. We've talked about purpose. But today, I want us to talk about what we stand for – in the lived experience of work.'

She invited the team to break into pairs and explore two questions:

1. What do we expect from our people now, beyond performance?

2. What can they expect from us in return?

The energy in the room shifted. At first, it felt conceptual. But quickly, it turned personal.

'We expect curiosity,' one leader said. 'But do we actually create safe spaces for questions?'

'We say we want innovation – but our risk systems still punish it.'

'We expect loyalty,' Leonie added. 'But are we giving people the growth, feedback and flexibility that today's employees value most?'

Sarah shared research from Great Place to Work (2022), which showed that high-performing cultures succeed not because of perks but because of how people are treated. Trust, autonomy, transparency and a sense of belonging were the real differentiators. These were the building blocks of the new deal – but only if they were felt consistently.

The group drafted a working statement:

The old deal said: 'Do the job, stay the course, earn your spot.'

The new deal says: 'Grow with us, challenge with us and we'll build something better – together.'

Angela had explained that the new deal wasn't a policy. It was a relational agreement – a living promise built through moments, expectations and actions.

Sarah proposed that they begin operationalizing the new deal by reviewing five key employee touchpoints:

1. Onboarding: rewriting the narrative from 'fitting in' to 'growing in'

2. Performance reviews: measuring development, not just delivery

3. Career paths: emphasizing mobility, contribution and learning

4. Exit interviews: framing departures as transitions, not betrayals

5. Team rituals: creating psychological safety and moments of connection

She could sense the shift. They were redesigning the employee experience to reflect the culture they wanted to grow. This wasn't just about fixing retention or updating comms. It was about building a company that kept its promises. Not just in what it delivered – but in how it made people *feel*.

From compliance to commitment – making the new deal stick

Two weeks later, Sarah and Leonie sat side-by-side in the Culture Lab – a reconfigured conference room where the People team had begun prototyping ideas. On the wall were sticky notes, experience maps and draft rewrites of employee touchpoints. But it was what was written across the whiteboard that made Sarah smile:

'How do we move from compliance to commitment?'

That was the real question.

They didn't want people to stay out of obligation. They wanted people to grow, stretch, contribute – and *choose* to stay.

Angela had been right: cultural change didn't happen through one big initiative. It happened through repetition, reinforcement and relationship.

'If the old deal was enforced through policy,' Sarah said, 'then the new deal has to be modelled through leadership.'

She circled the words.

The team had begun updating manager training to reflect this shift. Instead of checklists and KPIs alone, it now included emotional intelligence, coaching behaviours and storytelling – the kind that built connection, not just compliance.

They had introduced listening rituals too – not just surveys, but leader-directed conversations where employees could speak openly about what meaning looked like in their work. These forums weren't just for HR. They were for accountability.

Sarah referenced research from Gallup (2020), which showed that Millennials and Gen Z respond far better to coaches than to bosses – valuing feedback, career conversations and relational leadership over command-and-control. It was the missing skillset. Not only for managers but for the C-suite too.

She also drew on a model from The Alliance (Hoffman, Casnocha and Yeh, 2014), which framed the leader-employee relationship as a mutual growth pact. It offered a simple but powerful shift: view each employment chapter as a 'tour of duty' – a defined, purposeful period of contribution. When the mission was clear and the deal was transparent, performance and trust rose. And when it was time to move on, it wasn't failure. It was evolution.

Sarah leaned back, looking at the wall of sketches and ideas.

'We don't need a manifesto,' she said. 'We need evidence that we mean what we say.'

That would be the new deal. Not in words, but in experiences.

In who gets promoted. In what gets recognized. In how leaders show up when things are hard. They would close the chapter on the old deal not by tearing it down but by outgrowing it.

Together.

Final Reflection

The following Monday, Sarah paused outside the boardroom before a scheduled strategy review. She looked up at the large decal fixed to the wall just months earlier:

Powering the platforms that shape the future and help every person thrive.

It was still a powerful statement. But now, she saw it differently.

Purpose was not the problem. Translation was.

She thought about the recent culture sessions. The conversations with her team. The revised onboarding pilot. The first manager cohort going through the Meaning-Driven Leadership series. The small but meaningful steps they were taking to change the experience, not just the language.

This wasn't about signalling intent. It was about shaping systems. Modelling trust. Redesigning the contract of work – for relevance.

She stepped into the room and greeted her colleagues with quiet confidence. They weren't just writing a new deal, they were learning to live it.

Still, some leaders might ask: Does it really pay off? Is building a meaning-driven culture just a feel-good initiative, or can it deliver commercial advantage, measurable performance and real ROI?

Next, we will look how meaning pays.

Takeaways

- The old deal is no longer fit for purpose. The legacy model – loyalty in exchange for stability – has quietly collapsed. Employees now expect work to offer growth, contribution and emotional resonance (Rousseau, 1995; Meister and Willyerd, 2010).

- Psychological contracts matter. Unspoken expectations often drive employee experience more than formal policies. When those expectations break down, trust erodes and disengagement follows (Rousseau, 1995).

- The new deal is relational, not transactional. Employees are seeking purposeful, transparent relationships with their employers – not just pay for performance, but growth for contribution (Hoffman, Casnocha and Yeh, 2014; SHRM, 2022).

- Trust, autonomy and meaning are core to the new employee value proposition (EVP). Organizations that lead on meaning consistently outperform peers in retention, engagement and innovation (Frederick, 2021; Great Place to Work, 2022).

- Leaders must model the change. Employees take their cultural cues from leadership. If the new deal isn't reflected in feedback, recognition, promotions or manager behaviours, it becomes rhetoric. Gallup (2020) found that younger workers engage most with leaders who coach, not command.

Reflection Questions

1. What unspoken expectations (old deal assumptions) still shape your organization's systems – even if your stated values have evolved?

2. Where are you reinforcing compliance instead of cultivating commitment?

3. How is your EVP changing to reflect what employees value most today – beyond salary and stability?

4. In what ways are your managers and leaders still leading like bosses when employees need them to lead like coaches?

5. If someone looked at your recognition systems, promotion criteria and team rituals, would they see the new deal in action?

Chapter 4
Meaning pays – the ROI of meaningful work

'The soft stuff is the hard stuff.'
Roger Enrico, former CEO of PepsiCo

Summary

Here, we make the business case for meaningful work. Sarah begins to see that meaning isn't just a cultural or emotional driver – it's a strategic asset. As leaders search for levers to drive engagement, retention, innovation and performance, research consistently shows that meaning has measurable impact. Organizations that prioritize meaningful work don't just build better cultures – they build stronger businesses.

We explore global research from Gallup (Harter, Schmidt and Keyes, 2003), McKinsey (2021) and Harvard Business Review (2015) showing how employee engagement and meaningful work link directly to profitability, productivity, customer satisfaction and retention. Companies with strong, adaptive cultures significantly outperform peers (Kotter and Heskett, 2008; Sisodia, Wolfe and Sheth, 2007). Meaning-rich environments lead to higher shareholder returns, lower turnover and greater innovation (Edmans, 2012; Deloitte, 2019; Great Place to Work, 2022).

Sarah also starts to redefine how she and her team measure culture – not just through engagement scores, but through the leading indicators of meaning: autonomy, growth, purpose, connection and impact.

Meaning isn't just good for people. It's good for performance.

And in today's climate, where pressure on results is higher than ever, that matters more than ever.

A CEO's question – 'Does it pay?'

Sarah stood at the head of the table in NexusNova's monthly board meeting, watching her CFO flick through the new culture strategy slides.

She'd just finished presenting a roadmap for embedding meaning into leadership, team rituals and employee experience. The room was quiet. Not resistant – but cautious.

Finally, one board member cleared his throat.

'It all sounds… thoughtful. But does it pay?'

It was a fair question, one Sarah had asked herself more than once.

She turned to slide five, a graph showing engagement scores over time alongside productivity and retention metrics.

Angela had helped her build the business case. But she also knew numbers alone wouldn't shift minds. She needed to make meaning measurable.

'Here's what we know,' she began. 'When employees find their work meaningful, the results go far beyond morale. It impacts what they deliver, how long they stay and how they show up under pressure.'

She cited Gallup's longitudinal meta-analysis, which linked engagement to a cascade of business benefits – 21% higher profitability, 20% higher productivity and 59% lower turnover risk in high-engagement teams (Harter, Schmidt and Keyes, 2003).

And it wasn't just about engagement as a concept, it was about what drove it.

'Meaning is what fuels the discretionary effort every business leader wants,' she added. 'It's the difference between compliance and commitment.'

The room leaned in slightly. Sarah could feel it.

She flipped to a quote from the McKinsey Global Survey:

> *'Employees who find work meaningful are 75% more committed, 33% more productive and 49% less likely to leave.'*   (McKinsey and Company, 2021)

These weren't fringe findings. In a world of mounting talent shortages and investor scrutiny, they were fast becoming boardroom imperatives.

Sarah then referenced Sisodia, Wolfe and Sheth's (2007) study in *Firms of Endearment*, which showed that purpose-led, stakeholder-focused companies outperformed the SandP 500 by a factor of 8:1 over ten years. Culture wasn't soft. It was smart strategy.

She wrapped the section with a quote from Angela that had reframed her thinking:

'Meaning isn't a bonus feature of leadership. It's the engine of performance. And the companies who get that are already winning.'

From engagement to business impact

After the meeting, Sarah sat quietly in her office, reflecting on the board's response.

They hadn't pushed back. But they hadn't leaned in either. She recognized that look – interest without urgency.

'We need to make meaning feel essential,' she thought. 'Not just nice.'

She opened her laptop and pulled up Angela's internal culture deck – the one they'd been co-developing as part of the Meaning Over Purpose implementation. The next slide read:

Engagement is an outcome. Meaning is a driver.

That was the pivot she needed.

Over the past decade, 'engagement' had become the universal shorthand for culture health. But what Angela had helped her see – and what the research confirmed – was that engagement was only ever the *symptom*. The *cause* was whether people felt autonomy, mastery, purpose, connection and impact – the core drivers of meaningful work – in their daily work.

'We've been managing the temperature,' Angela had said. 'But ignoring the source of heat.'

Sarah pulled together a short document for her exec team. She titled it:

How Meaning Drives Business Value

The evidence was compelling:

- Companies with strong, adaptive cultures – many built on meaning and shared values – outperformed low-culture peers significantly over time. In their landmark study, Kotter and Heskett (2008) found that high-culture companies experienced 682% revenue growth versus 166% in low-culture counterparts over an 11-year period.

- The Great Place to Work Institute and Fortune report annually that the '100 Best Companies to Work For' consistently deliver higher stock returns, lower turnover and greater customer satisfaction than peers (Great Place to Work, 2022).

- Edmans (2012) analyzed employee satisfaction scores and firm value, showing that companies with highly satisfied workforces delivered higher long-term stock returns – even when controlling for other variables.

- Deloitte's (2019) *Economics of Purpose* report found that companies with clearly articulated and embedded purpose were 66% more likely to outperform competitors in profitability and brand trust.

This isn't just about employee happiness, Sarah wrote. *It's about sustained, measurable performance.* She added more:

- Employees who experience meaningful work are more intrinsically motivated, and that intrinsic motivation is a key driver of creativity and innovation (Amabile and Kramer, 2011).

- In Kruse's (2015) practical analysis of high-engagement organizations, meaningful work correlated with higher sales, fewer safety incidents and improved customer loyalty – outcomes every COO would care about.

- A meta-analysis by Reeve et al. (2018) showed that leaders who actively support autonomy – one of the Five Pillars – saw increases in both employee performance and psychological wellbeing.

- In a 2015 report from Harvard Business Review Analytic Services, over 70% of executives agreed that engagement directly impacted customer experience and operating margins – yet less than 30% felt confident they were measuring the right drivers (HBR Analytic Services, 2015).

Sarah exhaled slowly as she reviewed the stack. The pattern was undeniable. When people feel meaning, they deliver more. They stay longer. They solve better. They stretch further.

Meaning wasn't just about sentiment. It was about strategy. Angela had said it best: 'We've tried to out-perform our culture. What if we out-cultured our competitors instead?'

Sarah smiled. That was a phrase the board would remember.

Rethinking metrics – measuring what matters

The following week, Sarah gathered her executive team for a focused strategy session.

'We've built the case,' she began. 'Now we need to build the dashboard.'

Everyone nodded.

They'd spent the past few months rolling out new initiatives designed to embed meaning – more autonomy in project teams, a renewed focus on learning, leadership shadowing and redesigned recognition. But without measurement, it all risked becoming invisible.

Leonie was the first to speak. 'We track engagement. We track attrition. But those are lagging indicators. What are the leading indicators of meaning?'

That was the right question.

Angela had introduced them to a core principle early on:

What gets measured gets managed. But what gets felt gets remembered.

Sarah flipped open her notebook and pulled up a working draft she'd titled:

Meaning Metrics – What Matters Most

The model was built on four key domains:

Alignment, Growth, Connection, Resonance

Each was drawn from both research and experience:

- Alignment: the degree to which employees feel their values and role are connected to the organization's purpose (Pink, 2011; Deloitte, 2019)

- Growth: whether they believe they are learning, stretching and developing (Kruse, 2015)

- Connection: their sense of belonging, trust and meaningful relationships at work (Great Place to Work, 2022; Gallup, 2020)

- Resonance: the emotional energy they derive from their work – whether it feels worthwhile, energizing and personally fulfilling (Locke and Taylor, 1990; Edmans, 2012)

'These aren't "soft" things,' Sarah said. 'They're the soil everything else grows from.'

Angela had also shared that the best cultures tracked meaning experiences, not just meaning sentiment.

It wasn't about asking people if they were 'happy.' It was about understanding the conditions that helped them feel motivated, valued and inspired to perform.

Sarah outlined the first pilot they would run:

- Use focus groups to define what each Meaning Metric looked like in their context

- Introduce a monthly micro-survey asking just one question per domain

- Pair that data with storytelling – real examples from real teams of when meaning was present (and when it wasn't)

- Report the data monthly – alongside revenue, customer Net Promoter Score (NPS) and delivery metrics

'Meaning deserves a seat on the leadership dashboard,' she said.

As a driver. Because what they were really measuring wasn't emotion. It was energy.

Figure 6 presents the four domains of Meaning Metrics – a practical dashboard for measuring culture through what matters most to people.

RESONANCE

Emotional energy, fulfilment and pride

Does my work feel meaningful day to day?

CONNECTION

Belonging, inclusion and psychological safety

Do I feel safe, seen and connected?

ALIGNMENT

Personal alignment with purpose and values

Do I understand how my work matters?

GROWTH

Mastery, learning and personal growth

Am I progressing in ways that matter?

Figure 6: The Meaning Metrics model shows the four core domains of meaningful work: Alignment (values and purpose), Growth (learning and mastery), Connection (belonging and trust) and Resonance (emotional energy and fulfilment). When tracked consistently, they enable leaders to build high-trust, high-performance cultures.

Building the business case for meaning

The board presentation was three days away.

Sarah stood at the whiteboard in the strategy room, flanked by Leonie and two of her senior team leads. Around them were notes, frameworks and data points – the building blocks of the next big pitch.

But this wasn't a product launch or market expansion plan. It was a case for meaning made in the language the board understood: risk, growth and return.

'We've shown that meaning matters,' she said. 'Now we need to show that it pays – at the shareholder level.'

Leonie nodded. 'This is about business resilience. The return on culture is real – but we need to walk them through it logically.'

They began by mapping meaning-linked business outcomes across five areas:

1. Performance – higher productivity and quality of output

2. Retention – lower turnover and replacement cost

3. Innovation – greater discretionary effort and idea generation

4. Customer experience – improved empathy, trust and service

5. Brand equity – employer brand strength and investor confidence

'These are hard metrics,' Sarah said. 'We just need to connect the dots.'

She revisited the findings from HBR Analytic Services (2015): over 70% of executives agreed that employee engagement directly drives business outcomes like customer satisfaction and profitability – yet few felt confident in how to measure the drivers behind that engagement.

'That's our edge,' Sarah said. 'We're not just saying culture matters. We're showing how to track it.'

Angela had helped her shape the presentation around one key slide – a bold visual that reframed culture not as a cost but as a competitive edge.

At the top it read:

Meaning Drives Margin

It was simple – and strategic.

'We've been trained to measure performance through output,' Angela had explained, 'but meaning is what fuels input. It's the energy behind the effort. The reason behind the retention. The root system behind resilience.'

The diagram mapped six interconnected outcomes, each one grounded in hard data.

The diagram featured data from Gallup, McKinsey, Kotter and Great Place to Work – alongside internal NexusNova pilot results from their first Meaning Metrics dashboard trial. Sarah planned to use it as a pivot: from culture as cost, to culture as catalyst.

She also added a reference from Edmans (2012), whose research showed that companies with high employee satisfaction consistently outperformed their peers on long-term stock returns – even when controlling for firm size, industry and other variables.

Figure 7, Meaning Drives Margin, shows the six levers of performance fuelled by culture.

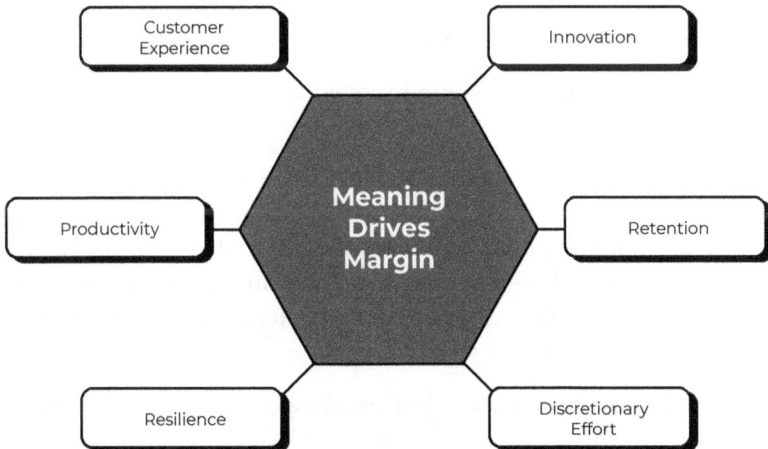

Figure 7: When meaning is embedded in leadership and culture it becomes a multiplier for performance. It activates six levers of business impact: productivity, retention, discretionary effort, resilience, innovation and customer experience. Leaders who scale meaning unlock not just loyalty, but energy and results.

'This is the shareholder story,' she said. 'Culture isn't the enemy of performance. It's the engine of it.'

As they finalized the deck, Sarah reflected on something Angela had told her during a working session: 'You're not pitching a culture initiative. You're redefining where your performance comes from.'

That was the business case. Not softer. Not slower. Smarter.

As Sarah prepared to present to the board, she knew this was the pivot. They weren't investing in 'culture.' They were investing in the conditions that drive performance from the inside out.

She remembered Angela's words: 'You're not pitching an initiative. You're redefining where your performance comes from.'

And that, she realized, was the real business case for meaningful work.

Final Reflection

Sarah stood by the window of her office as the city lights flickered on below. The presentation was done. The board had engaged with more curiosity than she expected – and less resistance than she feared.

What struck her most wasn't their approval.

It was the shift in the conversation.

They weren't asking *why* culture mattered anymore. They were asking *how* to scale it.

She thought about the journey so far – the metrics, the models, the research. But she also thought about the real moments: the team meeting where someone shared why a project mattered to them personally. The email from a new hire who said their onboarding felt 'human.' The frontline manager who redesigned a weekly meeting to start with one question: *Where did you feel proud this week?*

'That's ROI too,' she thought. 'It just takes longer to see on a spreadsheet.'

Meaning had moved from concept to capability. And now it was becoming currency. Not in place of profit – but as the path to it.

The wake-up call has sounded: the old deal is over, meaning is the new mandate, and it pays to pay attention. The question for leaders is no longer if we should invest in meaningful work. It's how to do it in a way that drives real impact, at scale.

That's where we go next.

Takeaways

- Meaningful work drives measurable business outcomes. Research consistently shows that when employees experience meaning, companies see higher performance, productivity and retention (Gallup, 2023; McKinsey and Company, 2021; Harter, Schmidt and Keyes, 2003).

- Purpose alone is not a performance strategy. Organizations must move beyond mission statements and translate purpose into daily experience through leadership behaviour, systems and metrics (Deloitte, 2019; Kotter and Heskett, 2008).

- High-performing cultures are high-trust, meaning-rich cultures. Companies that prioritize meaning and shared values outperform peers in shareholder returns, customer satisfaction and innovation (Sisodia, Wolfe and Sheth, 2007; Great Place to Work, 2022; Edmans, 2012).

- Meaning Metrics create actionable insight. Alignment, Growth, Connection and Resonance are leading indicators of discretionary effort and emotional commitment – both essential for sustained success (Pink, 2011; Reeve et al., 2018; Locke and Taylor, 1990).

- Meaning is not a soft initiative: it's a strategic advantage. In a world of volatility, people are the performance system. Organizations that activate meaning don't just retain talent – they unlock its full potential (HBR Analytic Services, 2015).

Reflection Questions

1. What business outcomes in your organization are most influenced by culture – and how clearly do you measure those links?

2. Where might your organization be measuring engagement without tracking the deeper drivers of meaning?

3. Which of the four Meaning Metrics (Alignment, Growth, Connection, Resonance) is strongest in your culture – and which needs investment?

4. How is your leadership team held accountable for the culture they create – not just the results they deliver?

5. What would it look like to move meaning from philosophy to performance metric – and what's the first step?

PART II
LEADING WITH MEANING – BUILDING A HIGH-PERFORMANCE CULTURE

Sarah stood in front of a whiteboard at NexusNova's leadership offsite, a marker in her hand and a new kind of energy in the room.

This time, she wasn't reviewing financial targets or product timelines. She was drawing a model – the Five Pillars – and inviting her executive team to design with her.

'Let's stop talking about culture,' she said. 'Let's start building it.'

This was the turning point.

They had already named the issue – the Purpose-to-Meaning Gap. They had confronted the cost of disengagement. They had seen why the old leadership contract was no longer fit for the future. Part I of this journey had woken them up.

Now came the real work: reimagining the organization from the inside out.

In this section of the book, the focus shifts from insight to action. Together, we'll explore how leaders like Sarah and her team begin designing a culture of meaning not through inspirational speeches, but through structure, behaviour and measurable change.

You'll meet:

- The Five Pillars – the building blocks of meaningful work, grounded in psychology, motivation theory and lived experience

- The Meaningful Work Ecosystem – a practical model for embedding meaning at every level of the organization

- The Lead with Meaning playbook – a new behavioural standard for leaders, anchored in trust, purpose and inclusion

- Meaning Metrics – a dashboard to measure culture with the same rigour used for performance

This is where theory becomes architecture.

Angela's frameworks are no longer ideas. They're tools used by real leaders in real systems to create real results.

For Sarah, this was a period of rapid experimentation – and equally rapid reflection. Not everything worked. But what mattered was that they were no longer asking if meaning belonged in the business. They were asking how to make it the business.

So if Part I asked, *Why does meaning matter?*

Part II asks, *What does meaning look like in action?*

And the answer is closer – and more tangible – than many leaders think.

Let's build.

Chapter 5
The Five Pillars of
Meaningful Work – from
insight to action

'An organization's ability to learn and translate
that learning into action rapidly, is the ultimate
competitive advantage.'
Jack Welch

Summary

Now we move from insight to action. Sarah begins to understand that meaning isn't an abstract concept or one-time campaign – it's built through daily experience. And that experience is shaped by five powerful drivers: Autonomy, Mastery, Purpose, Connection and Impact.

We introduce the Five Pillars of Meaningful Work, a practical framework grounded in psychology, motivation theory and real-world culture design. Together, these pillars form the foundation of the employee experience – and the basis for sustained engagement, energy and commitment.

Each pillar is a universal driver of meaning at work – grounded in decades of motivation theory and organizational psychology. Together, they form the design principles for energizing individuals, teams and leaders.

For Sarah and her leadership team, the Five Pillars become more than a framework. They become a language – a way to diagnose, design and deliver meaning at scale.

Where meaning lives – shaping the daily experience

Sarah sat in the back of the room, notebook open, silently observing her executive team in a strategy planning session.

On the surface, everything was smooth. The discussion was focused. Slide decks were clear. Timelines were aligned. But something about the conversation left her uneasy.

No one seemed curious. No one had smiled in over 30 minutes. The energy was flat – not because anything was wrong, but because nothing felt alive.

As the meeting adjourned, she jotted down a single line: *We are clear – but not connected.*

Later that evening, she brought it up with Angela during a check-in call. They'd been working closely since launching the Meaning Over Purpose blueprint across NexusNova's leadership programmes.

Angela didn't hesitate.

'Meaning doesn't live in the big moments. It lives in the daily experience. If people don't feel autonomy, growth, connection or impact, the purpose becomes noise.'

Sarah nodded. She'd seen it firsthand. It wasn't that people didn't believe in the company's mission. It was that they couldn't always see themselves in it – especially in the press of everyday work.

She opened her notebook to a page she had bookmarked several times.

The Five Pillars of Meaningful Work

Angela had shared this framework during an offsite. It had stayed with Sarah ever since – not because it was catchy, but because it was true. When those five elements were present, people lit up. When they were missing, even the most talented individuals eventually drifted.

- Autonomy
- Mastery
- Purpose
- Connection
- Impact

Each pillar was grounded in decades of research. Autonomy and Mastery traced back to self-determination theory (Deci and Ryan, 2000), which showed that intrinsic motivation – the kind that fuels sustainable engagement – arises when people feel capable and self-directed. Without those, performance becomes performative.

Sarah thought back to her early years as a leader. She had focused on clarity, systems, consistency. But the leaders she admired most had focused on something else – energy. And that energy came from people feeling they could shape their work, not just execute it.

Angela had also shared the work of Hackman and Oldham (1976), whose job characteristics model demonstrated that when work was designed to offer variety, significance and autonomy, employees reported significantly higher motivation and performance. Meaning, in other words, was designed into the day – not delivered in keynote speeches.

Sarah turned the page.

The next pillar was Purpose – the most familiar of all, yet still the most misunderstood. People didn't need purpose to be lofty. They needed it to be personal. Studies by Wrzesniewski et al. (1997) had shown that people who saw their jobs as part of a broader calling – regardless of role – experienced higher meaning, commitment and wellbeing. It wasn't about the job title. It was about the lens.

Next: Connection. Sarah paused here.

This was the one she knew they were struggling with post-pandemic. Even as hybrid ways of working had stabilized, the sense of belonging had not. According to Edmondson (1999), psychological safety – the belief that it's safe to speak up, take risks and show up authentically – was essential for learning and collaboration. Without it, teams might function – but they would never thrive.

Angela had layered this insight with Brené Brown's work on vulnerability and trust, reminding Sarah that connection wasn't just about *who* was in the room – but *how* they showed up (Brown, 2012). And whether people believed they were safe to do so.

She turned to the final pillar: Impact. The most powerful – and most often overlooked.

Angela had shared a study by Adam Grant (2007) showing that when call centre workers met the people who benefitted from their fundraising, their performance more than doubled. Why? Because impact had been made visible. That small moment had reminded them that their work mattered.

Sarah looked down at the five words again.

Autonomy. Mastery. Purpose. Connection. Impact.

They weren't just pillars of meaning. They were levers of culture.

And they were her new diagnostic for leadership.

See Figure 8, The Five Pillars of Meaningful Work, for the foundational drivers of meaning and how they show up in the daily experience of work.

As the session wrapped, Sarah paused in front of the flipchart where the Five Pillars had been explored.

'We know what each pillar means,' she said. 'But let's make it even clearer. What does it look like – and what does it sound like – when meaning is present? And what happens when it's not?'

Angela nodded.

'That's how we make it actionable.'

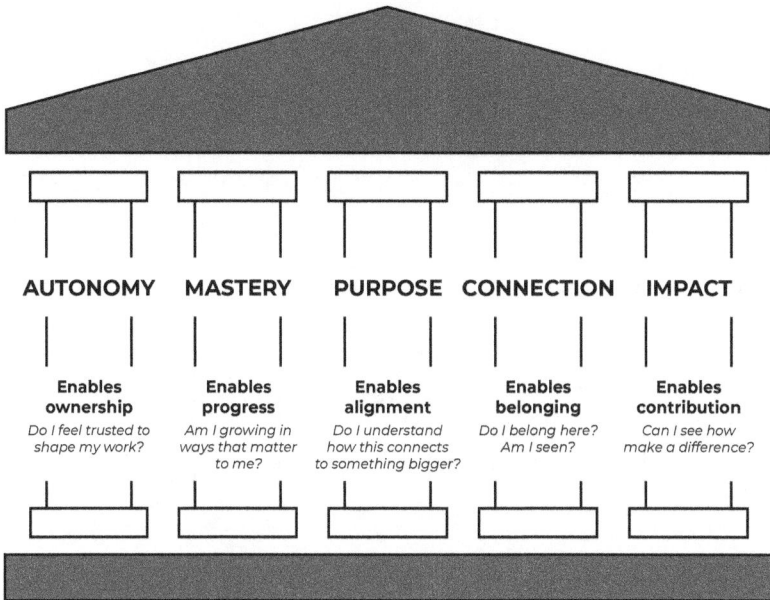

Figure 8: The Five Pillars of Meaningful Work – Autonomy, Mastery, Purpose, Connection and Impact – shape how people experience meaning in their work. The more present each pillar is, the smaller the meaning gap becomes. While all Five Pillars matter, people experience and prioritize them differently depending on values, life stage and context.

The team created a table together – simple, but powerful. A quick reference to help leaders translate each pillar into behaviour and experience.

The Five Pillars in practice – seeing the signals

Figure 9 brings the Five Pillars to life – contrasting what each looks like when actively present versus when meaning is missing.

Sarah made a note in bold at the top of her page:

> 'Leaders don't need to fix everything – but they need to **notice** when meaning is missing.'

AUTONOMY   MASTERY   PURPOSE   CONNECTION   IMPACT

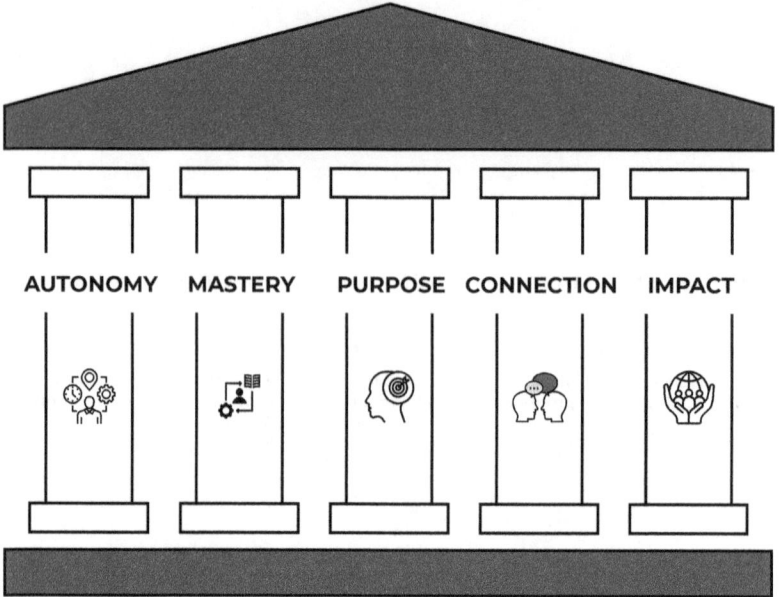

When present	When missing
Individuals can see tangible outcomes of their efforts and feel their contribution matters.	People feel disconnection from results, low motivation 'Does any of this even matter?'
Teams feel like communities; psychological safety and belonging are strong.	Individuals experience isolation, exclusion, silo mentality 'I don't feel seen or supported.'
Individuals clearly understand how their work connects to a larger mission.	People feel disengaged, apathy, cynical 'Why am I doing this?'
People are growing, learning and developing new skills; strength and support are balanced.	Organizations see stagnation, 'quiet quitting', high-potential talent leaving, 'I'm stuck'.
People feel trusted to own their work and make decisions; they have flexibility and voice.	People suffer micromanagement, results in low initiative, passive compliance. 'I just do as I'm told.'

Figure 9: Each pillar of meaningful work is either present in daily experience or missing. This visual helps leaders recognize the signals: when meaning is active, people feel energized, connected and proud. When it's absent, performance may continue but engagement, resilience and commitment begin to erode.

Pillar by pillar – what meaningful work really looks like

Sarah stood at the front of the leadership retreat, marker in hand, the words *Meaningful Work* written across the flipchart.

'Today,' she said, 'we're going to stop talking about meaning as a concept – and start learning how to lead it.'

She flipped the page and wrote the first pillar in bold:

1. Autonomy – the freedom to shape how work happens

'Let's start with Autonomy,' she said. 'Not independence. Not anarchy. But the freedom to contribute with agency.'

Sarah explained that autonomy wasn't about removing structure – it was about removing unnecessary control. The freedom to influence your approach, your process and sometimes even your priorities was one of the clearest predictors of motivation and engagement.

Deci and Ryan's self-determination theory (2000) had long established autonomy as a foundational need for human flourishing. When people feel micromanaged, motivation dies. When they feel trusted to think and act, performance and ownership increase.

Angela had put it simply: 'Autonomy is how people feel powerfully human at work.'

Sarah shared how one of her engineering teams had recently piloted a sprint model where developers could shape not only how but what they worked on for a portion of the cycle. Creativity soared. Collaboration deepened.

She asked the group, 'Where are we unintentionally controlling when we could be trusting?'

She invited each leader to review where decision rights were concentrated and which could be redistributed. Small shifts, like letting teams shape how sprint goals were tackled, or choosing meeting formats created outsized gains in ownership and morale.

2. Mastery – the drive to grow and make progress

Sarah moved to the second pillar: Mastery.

'This one,' she said, 'is often confused with ambition. But mastery isn't about climbing the ladder. It's about feeling you're improving. That your work is developing you, not just consuming you.'

The team reflected.

She referenced Csikszentmihalyi's (1990) concept of flow – that deeply focused state where challenge meets skill and time disappears. Flow states are most likely to occur when people are doing work that stretches them just enough to stay engaged, but not so much they feel overwhelmed.

Sarah checked her notebook and cited Amabile and Kramer (2011), whose research in *The Progress Principle* showed that the single greatest driver of motivation at work was a sense of daily progress – even small wins.

'It doesn't matter how senior someone is,' she said. 'Everyone needs to feel like they're getting better at something.' Sarah encouraged each leader to open 1:1s with growth-focused questions and celebrate small wins in team meetings. She suggested they could also build in learning time, such as 10% unstructured, curiosity-led space per quarter, to create energy without needing permission.

Mastery was about movement. And leaders could cultivate it by designing stretch opportunities, giving feedback focused on growth and recognizing the journey – not just the result.

3. Purpose – the experience of personal significance

Next: Purpose.

'In the Five Pillars framework, purpose doesn't mean an organization's mission statement or brand promise. It means the felt experience of significance in the personal "why" behind daily work. Purpose, in this context, is about how people make sense of what they do and why it matters to them. That distinction is essential because corporate purpose can be beautifully stated, but if people don't feel connected to it, meaning won't follow.'

Sarah paused here, knowing this pillar could easily become abstract.

'Purpose doesn't mean changing the world,' she said. 'It means understanding why your work matters – to you.'

She shared a reflection from a customer service rep who had said during a listening circle: 'I'm not just logging tickets. I'm helping someone else get their work back on track. That matters to me.'

That, Angela had said, was the real work of purpose: connecting the task to meaning.

She pointed to Wrzesniewski et al. (1997), whose research distinguished between seeing your job as a task, a career or a calling. The same job could be experienced differently based on the meaning people attributed to it – and leaders could help shape that attribution.

Sarah asked her leaders, 'Where are we helping people connect their role to the bigger picture – and where are we accidentally stripping the purpose out of it?'

She continued: 'One small change we could make is to add a *Why this matters* section to project briefs and team updates. Or encourage team members to write their own answers, linking the task to what motivates them personally.'

4. Connection – the feeling of belonging and psychological safety

The fourth pillar was the most fragile.

Sarah wrote: Connection.

'This is where many organizations are struggling right now,' she said. 'Because hybrid working has increased flexibility – but it's also weakened the glue between people.'

She quoted Amy Edmondson (1999), who defined psychological safety as a shared belief that the team is safe for interpersonal risk-taking. Without it, teams grow silent. Innovation stalls. People show up, but not fully.

Connection was about more than friendship. It was about trust. Inclusion. Belonging. Recognition.

Angela had challenged her team once with a simple but uncomfortable question: 'Who in your organization feels invisible?'

Sarah also highlighted research by Dutton, Roberts and Bednar (2010), who showed that meaningful work is often constructed through positive interactions and identity-affirming relationships. She proposed starting team meetings with three-minute check-ins as personal prompts that invite presence. She also encouraged leaders to track airtime and inclusion patterns: who speaks, who gets interrupted and who isn't being heard. Finally, they designed new rituals like 'Close the Loop' as end-of-project reviews where teams could hear how their work helped others. Sarah also asked each leader to share one impact story at every town hall, spotlighting roles that often went unseen.

Connection isn't just a nice bonus. It is how meaning is sustained.

5. Impact – the sense that what I do makes a difference

Finally, Sarah turned to the last pillar: Impact.

This, she said, was where meaning often came alive – or disappeared altogether.

Angela had shared Adam Grant's (2007) landmark study of call centre workers. One group simply made calls. The second group met a student whose scholarship they were fundraising for. The result? The second group raised 171% more money. They weren't told their work mattered. They *felt* it.

Sarah shared her own version: a frontline employee who had recently joined a project debrief session and cried when they heard how their work had directly contributed to a successful client rescue mission. 'I didn't know I mattered like that,' they had said.

'Impact isn't always visible,' Sarah told the room. 'But our job as leaders is to make it visible.'

She paused, looking at the group of leaders around her.

'These pillars are how people know they matter. They're how we build meaning into the experience – not just the words.'

The room was still. Heads nodded slowly.

And in that moment, the pillars weren't just a framework anymore.

They were the foundation.

Diagnosing the gaps – what's missing and where

A week later, Sarah stood in front of a group of 30 NexusNova leaders – directors and senior managers handpicked from across the business.

This was the Meaning Lab: a new pilot programme designed to explore how meaning was showing up – or not – in the employee experience.

Angela facilitated the session, opening with a simple prompt:

'If you had to rate each of the Five Pillars of Meaningful Work in your team today, where would you score high – and where might you be unintentionally eroding meaning?'

The group moved into small clusters, each one handed a worksheet with five sliders – one for each pillar. They were asked to reflect on three questions per domain:

1. Where is this pillar actively designed into your team culture?

2. Where is it assumed or taken for granted?

3. Where is it missing entirely?

What followed surprised Sarah. The group didn't speak in corporate language. They spoke as people. And the honesty was sharp.

- 'We over-manage timelines. Autonomy is low.'

- 'Mastery gets talked about in promotion interviews but nowhere else.'

- 'Connection is strong in-person. Remote, it vanishes.'

- 'Impact is invisible. My team only hears about problems, never outcomes.'

Angela nodded as the feedback flowed, referencing Amabile and Kramer (2011) again: 'Even small wins – when made visible – can dramatically boost engagement.'

In the plenary session, Leonie shared a thought that resonated with the whole group: 'I think we've all assumed that if people are performing, they must be fine. But that doesn't mean they feel meaning. We've never measured for it – so we've never managed it.'

Sarah underlined that in her notebook.

That afternoon, the group began building a shared map of their cultural hotspots – places where meaning was flourishing; and blind spots – where meaning was being drained silently through process, pressure or neglect.

In one exercise, they overlaid recent employee pulse survey results with the Five Pillars, adding narrative comments from exit interviews and team retrospectives.

The pattern was immediate:

- Autonomy was lowest in project support functions – where KPIs were tight and creativity was discouraged.

- Mastery was missing in stable but stagnant teams – those praised for efficiency, but with little learning stretch.

- Purpose was fragmented – strong at the top, vague at the front lines.

- Connection varied wildly by manager – some teams had rituals and rhythms, others did not.

- Impact was near-invisible – not because it wasn't there, but because it wasn't communicated.

'This is your cultural fingerprint,' Angela said. 'And it tells a story.'

Sarah stood at the wall of sticky notes, graphs and heat maps. She felt a sense of gravity – and clarity.

'If this is what's true,' she said, 'then this is where we lead next.'

These insights pointed to a deeper truth: meaningful work doesn't scale through passion alone; it scales through systems.
(See Appendix 3: Personal Meaningful Work Inventory for a guided exercise you can use individually or with your team.)

Designing for meaning – leadership in action

Two weeks later, the NexusNova leadership team came together again – this time with a new brief:

'If we know where meaning is missing,' Sarah said, 'then let's start building it in.'

The room was energized.

Instead of strategy decks, the tables were covered in flip charts, coloured pens and sticky notes. This wasn't a planning session – it was a design sprint.

Each team chose one pillar to focus on and was asked to prototype three simple experiments: low-cost, high-impact changes they could trial over the next 30 days.

Designing for Autonomy

One team focused on Autonomy, recognizing that in their function, decision rights were concentrated at the top. They proposed a new practice – 'Decision Rounds' – bi-weekly sessions where frontline team members were invited to shape priorities for the next sprint. The manager's role would be to facilitate, not dictate.

'We're not giving up accountability,' one director said. 'We're building confidence through ownership.'

Angela reminded the group that autonomy doesn't mean detachment. It means empowered contribution. Research by Reeve et al. (2018) confirmed that autonomy-supportive leadership significantly boosts motivation, performance and psychological wellbeing.

Designing for Mastery

Another group took on Mastery.

They created a 'Growth Moments' initiative – inviting every manager to open their 1:1s with one new question: *Where are you growing right now?*

It seemed small, but Angela had shared data from *The Progress Principle* (Amabile and Kramer, 2011), showing that even small acknowledgements of development lead to sustained motivation.

They also recommended adding a 'Learning Highlight' slide to monthly team meetings, where someone would share a recent mistake or insight that propelled them forward.

Designing for Purpose

The Purpose group focused on communication. They proposed redesigning project briefs to include one new section:

Why this work matters to us, to others and to the mission.

This drew directly from Wrzesniewski et al. (1997), whose work showed that people are more engaged when they see their work as a *calling*, not just a task – and when they connect their role to something larger than themselves.

Designing for Connection

The team exploring Connection acknowledged that hybrid work had eroded daily interaction. Their prototype: 'Check-in Circles'. Once a week, each team would dedicate the first ten minutes of a meeting to a personal prompt – not work-related, but designed to build empathy and trust.

Angela reminded the group of Edmondson's (1999) research on psychological safety: when people feel safe to show up fully, collaboration and learning improve. Connection wasn't just about being social; it was about trust, belonging and knowing your presence mattered.

Designing for Impact

Finally, the Impact team recommended a practice called 'Close the Loop'. Every project team would commit to circling back with frontline contributors to show the outcomes of their work through stories, client feedback or end-of-project reviews.

Sarah loved this one.

'It's easy to forget,' she said, 'that most people never hear the ending of the story they helped write.'

She referenced Grant's (2007) work again – how making impact visible changes how people feel about their contribution, their energy and their resilience.

The team left that session not just aligned but committed.

Each experiment would be trialled, measured and refined over the next quarter. And meaning, for the first time, was no longer an aspiration. It was a design principle.

'We're not waiting for people to find meaning,' Sarah said. 'We're building the conditions for it.'

Final Reflection

Later that night, Sarah returned to the wall in her office where she'd pinned up early notes on the Meaning Over Purpose journey. The original diagrams were still there – Purpose Gap, Meaning Gap, the Meaning Over Purpose blueprint.

But now, one new page stood out above the rest:

Autonomy. Mastery. Purpose. Connection. Impact.
Five words. Five forces. Five responsibilities of leadership. Not as a checklist – but as a design brief.

She thought back to the early days of the business when purpose had been the north star. They'd built vision decks. Written values. Crafted statements. But what had changed – what was changing – was the understanding that meaning wasn't declared. It was cultivated. Through leadership behaviours. Through feedback rituals. Through quiet moments of recognition, agency and trust.

And if those moments were designed well? Then people wouldn't just understand the purpose of the organization. They'd feel their own purpose inside it.

Armed with these Five Pillars of intrinsic motivation, the next challenge was clear: how to weave them into the fabric of the organization. Not as isolated efforts or individual leadership styles, but as part of the daily operating system visible in systems, rituals and behaviours at every level. That's where the Meaningful Work Ecosystem comes in and where we turn to next.

Takeaways

- Meaning is designed through daily experience. It does not live in values posters or purpose statements. It is built – or broken – through micro-moments of autonomy, development, recognition and belonging (Amabile and Kramer, 2011; Edmondson, 1999).

- The Five Pillars of Meaningful Work are deeply research-backed. Autonomy and Mastery reflect self-determination theory (Deci and Ryan, 2000). Purpose aligns with job calling theory (Wrzesniewski et al., 1997). Connection draws from psychological safety (Edmondson, 1999) and relational identity theory (Dutton et al., 2010). Impact connects to prosocial motivation and visibility of outcomes (Grant, 2007).

- Small changes drive meaningful impact. Leaders don't need grand strategies to build meaning. Instead, they must redesign daily interactions and systems to activate the conditions for meaning – across hiring, onboarding, team meetings and performance reviews (Reeve et al., 2018; Brown, 2012).

- Meaning is not just about feelings – it's about fuel. When people feel meaning, they work smarter, stay longer and contribute more. The Five Pillars are performance infrastructure (Hackman and Oldham, 1976; Csikszentmihalyi, 1990).

- Designing for meaning is now a leadership responsibility. When organizations rely on purpose alone, they create disengagement. When they embed the Five Pillars into leadership practice, they close the Purpose-to-Meaning Gap and unlock culture as a business advantage.

Reflection Questions

1. Where in your organization is one of the Five Pillars strong – and where is one being unintentionally eroded?

2. As a leader, which of the Five Pillars are you most confident in role-modelling – and which one do you need to grow?

3. How might you redesign a routine team ritual (e.g., stand-up, 1:1, project debrief) to embed one or more of the pillars more intentionally?

4. Are your people systems – performance, recognition, learning – enabling the Five Pillars or blocking them?

5. What would shift if your organization treated meaning as a strategic system – not a side effect?

Chapter 6
The Meaningful Work Ecosystem – how to embed meaning at scale

'The leader is one who can organize the experience of the group... in order to advance the purpose of the group.'
Mary Parker Follett

Summary

We now transition from the individual experience of meaning and ask a more complex leadership question: *How do you embed meaning at scale?*

Sarah begins to understand that it's not enough for a few teams to 'get it.' If meaning is to become a cultural foundation and not just a personal experience, it must be designed into the ecosystem: through roles, rituals, leadership behaviours and organizational systems.

We introduce the Meaningful Work Ecosystem, Angela's multi-level framework for activating meaning at the individual, team, leadership and organizational levels. Inspired by ecological theory (Bronfenbrenner, 1977) and system design thinking, it provides leaders with a blueprint for embedding meaning, not just encouraging it.

This model builds on – and moves beyond – previous research in the field. Scholars like Lips-Wiersma and Morris (2009), Bailey and Madden (2016) and Rosso et al. (2010) have explored both the inner dimensions of meaningful work and the organizational conditions that shape it, from values alignment and moral complexity to role design and culture. Their work has helped map the psychological, relational and ethical terrain of meaning at work. Angela's Meaningful Work Ecosystem approach honours and extends these foundations by offering a systemic design framework: one that translates theory into actionable structures, rhythms and practices that can scale across complex organizations.

We also draw from psychological safety (Edmondson and Lei, 2014), leadership impact (Ulrich and Ulrich, 2010) and positive organization design (Cameron and Spreitzer, 2012) to make the case that meaning is not just a mindset – it's a product of structure, expectation and intentional leadership.

For Sarah and her team, the Meaningful Work Ecosystem becomes more than a framework. It becomes the missing operating model for turning purpose into practice and meaning into a competitive advantage.

From pockets of meaning to embedded culture

Sarah leaned against the glass wall of her office, scanning the Post-it® notes still pinned from last week's Meaning Lab session. Each one represented a breakthrough – a pattern spotted, a blind spot named, one of the Five Pillars brought to life.

Teams had begun redesigning feedback loops to build Mastery, rewriting project briefs to reinforce Purpose and experimenting with storytelling to surface Impact.

There was momentum. She could feel it.

But she also knew something else. 'We're still relying on individual insight,' she thought. 'What happens when the champions leave?'

Angela had warned her about this in their last debrief.

'You've activated meaning in pockets,' Angela had said. 'But if it's not embedded in the system, it won't last. Meaning needs structure – and that's where the Meaningful Work Ecosystem comes in.'

Sarah wrote one phrase in her notebook and circled it: *The shift now is from culture by chance to culture by design.*

This was the next frontier in the journey. They had introduced the Five Pillars (Chapter 5) and leaders were beginning to activate them in daily experience. They had piloted Meaning Metrics (Chapter 4) to track how meaning showed up in the lived reality of work.

But none of this would be sustained over the long term unless the organization itself – the structures, expectations, behaviours and rhythms – reinforced those conditions systemically.

Angela had called it the Meaningful Work Ecosystem – a multi-level design architecture that helps organizations embed meaning across four interconnected levels:

1. Individual – how people understand and experience meaning personally

2. Team – how groups foster connection, safety and shared values

3. Leadership – how leaders model meaning through their actions and decisions

4. Organization – how systems, strategy and culture reinforce or erode meaning at scale

The idea wasn't just intuitive – it was supported by decades of theory.

Bronfenbrenner's (1977) ecological model had long argued that human development is shaped by layered environments, from the personal to the systemic. Similarly, meaningful work is experienced not in isolation, but in context. Rosso et al. (2010) outlined key pathways to meaning that flow through job design, leadership, values alignment and workplace culture.

Katie Bailey and Marjolein Lips-Wiersma, in their respective research, also emphasized that meaning isn't just a personal pursuit – it's affected by structural conditions, team dynamics and leadership climate (Bailey and Madden, 2016; Lips-Wiersma and Morris, 2009).

'Meaning is ecological,' Angela had said. 'It doesn't stick unless the environment supports it.'

Sarah could now see it clearly: the work they had done on the Five Pillars was necessary – but not sufficient. If the Meaningful Work Ecosystem didn't support those pillars, they would collapse under pressure.

'We need more than isolated champions,' she thought. 'We need an environment that holds meaning together.'

In Figure 10, The Meaningful Work Ecosystem shows how meaning must be embedded at four levels – individual, team, leadership and organization.

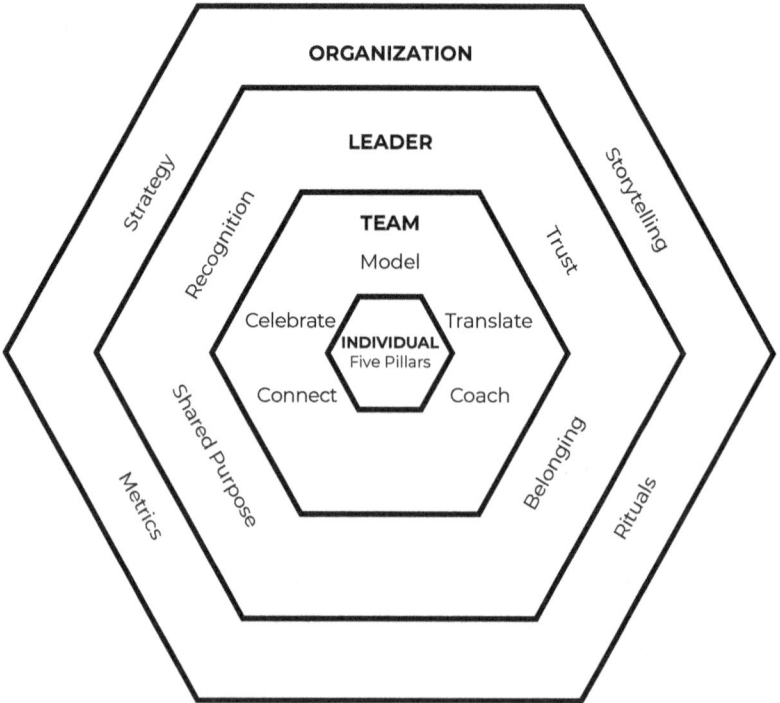

Figure 10: The Meaningful Work Ecosystem offers a multi-level framework for embedding meaning into daily experience across individuals, teams, leaders and organizational systems. Meaning is sustained through intentional alignment, not just at the top, but across every level of the organization.

Four levels of design – the architecture of meaning

The team was now ready to go beyond values and behaviours. Angela had prepared a deeper framework – one that would allow NexusNova to embed the Five Pillars through organizational architecture. She stood at the front of the leadership team retreat and drew four concentric rings on a flipchart.

'Meaning is built in layers,' she said. 'If we don't design all four levels intentionally, we rely on charisma and memory. That doesn't scale. What does scale is a system.'

We've already explored the Five Pillars – Autonomy, Mastery, Purpose, Connection and Impact,' Angela said. 'Now we need to examine where and how those pillars are supported – or undermined – across your organization. That's what this model does.'

She labelled each ring as she spoke:

1. Individual

2. Team

3. Leadership

4. Organization

'This,' she said, 'is your Meaningful Work Ecosystem.'

Sarah watched as the room leaned forward. Everyone recognized the truth in what Angela was saying – and in what they'd experienced: the brilliant team culture that vanished when a manager left, energy that collapsed under system pressure, engagement that disappeared after reorgs.

Angela continued.

'You've started designing for meaning using the Five Pillars. But unless your systems support them – at every level – they won't hold under pressure.'

1. Individual – personal meaning and identity

The core of the Ecosystem is the individual – the personal lens through which employees interpret their experience. At this level, the Five Pillars aren't experienced as a framework, they're felt as a lived reality. For one person, it might be the autonomy to shape how they approach a task. For another, it's the increasing sense of mastery as they grow in a new role. These moments may appear small but they're not insignificant. Together, they shape how someone answers the question: Does my work still reflect who I am, and who I want to become?

When the Five Pillars show up in ways that align with personal values, identity, and strengths, meaning becomes internalized, not imposed. That's why the individual is at the core of the ecosystem. But the organization must make space for these to flourish.

This is where Alignment and Resonance – two of your core Meaning Metrics – are most critical. Do employees feel they can bring their full selves to work? Are their personal values reflected in the work they do?

Angela shared with the leadership team how research by Dik, Byrne and Steger (2013), who showed that meaningful work arises when people feel they can express their values and use their strengths in pursuit of a shared goal, reinforces the value of these metrics. Similarly, Park and Peterson (2008) demonstrated that when employees use their signature strengths in their role, wellbeing and performance increase.

'If your job erases your identity,' Angela said, 'you'll never feel meaning.'

2. Team – norms, safety and belonging

Next was the team – the most emotionally powerful unit of organizational life.

Angela turned to the group. 'Let me ask you something,' she said. 'If someone feels respected in their team, how much do company values really matter?'

The room was quiet. 'Team culture either reinforces meaning – or replaces it.'

At this level, the Connection and Mastery pillars come to life. Meaning is shaped by norms, rituals, psychological safety and shared purpose. Research by Edmondson and Lei (2014) confirms that teams with high psychological safety innovate more, retain more and recover faster from failure. Meaning Metrics like Connection and Growth are strongly shaped at the team level – through rituals, safety and shared ownership of learning.

Sarah saw it clearly now: even in high-performing teams, meaning can quietly erode if people don't feel safe, seen or stretched.

This is where meaning is felt, she wrote. *Not in the values on the wall – but in the everyday habits of the team.*
(Use Appendix 4: Team Meaningfulness Health Check to guide ongoing conversations and spot areas needing attention.)

3. Leadership – modelling meaning through behaviour

The third layer was leadership.

'You can't scale meaning,' Angela said, 'if your leaders are modelling performance without purpose.'

Here, the Five Pillars and Meaning Metrics converge – leaders reinforce meaning not just by what they say, but by what they recognize, measure and model.

Angela cited Ulrich and Ulrich (2010), who argue that the most enduring organizations are those whose leaders consistently build meaning into conversations, decisions and development. Kahn (1992) also emphasized the role of leaders in enabling 'psychological presence' – the ability to show up fully at work.

Sarah thought back to her earlier habits: clear targets, quick reviews and systems optimized for speed – but not always for meaning. She realized now that leadership needed to hold the emotional architecture of the culture. Not just the targets.

This was where meaning either scaled – or stalled.

4. Organization – systems, strategy and culture infrastructure

Finally, Angela moved to the outer ring: organization.

'If you want meaning to be sustainable,' she said, 'you must design for it. At this level, culture becomes durable,' she said. 'This is where Meaning Metrics need to be integrated into your performance dashboards, your strategic reviews and your people systems. That means culture isn't just behaviours; it's systems alignment.'

Angela referenced an HBR article by Beer, Finnström and Schrader (2016), which argues that most leadership training fails not because of bad content but because the surrounding organization (processes, incentives, structure) stays the same.

Sarah underlined the insight in her notes: *Meaning will only survive if our systems carry it – not just our intentions.*

Angela also highlighted Thompson and Bunderson (2003), who found that employees form ideological psychological contracts – expecting organizations to act in ways that align with shared values. When those expectations are violated, even if unintentionally, people withdraw trust and motivation.

This level activates Purpose, Impact and long-term Growth. From performance systems to onboarding. From recognition to resource allocation.

'This is how meaning becomes infrastructure,' Angela said.

Sarah looked at the four levels again. It was elegant. It was clear. And it explained what had always felt like the missing link.

They hadn't failed to communicate meaning. They'd failed to design for it.

Angela introduced a systemic culture mapping tool to identify what rituals and systems reinforced the Five Pillars. *(Use Appendix 2: Meaningful Work Cultural Embedding Audit to apply this lens across your own organizational ecosystem.)*

Mapping the ecosystem – from insight to action

Two weeks after the retreat, Sarah stood in the Culture and People war room – a space now affectionately dubbed the 'Meaning Lab'. The walls were lined with maps, diagrams and quotes from employees across every part of the business.

At the centre of the room was the visual they'd all rallied around: the Meaningful Work Ecosystem.

The Meaningful Work Hexagon had shown them the six strategic capability areas for meaningful work. The Five Pillars had revealed the motivational drivers. Now, the Meaningful Work Ecosystem tied it all together – showing where meaning lived and what conditions either enabled or blocked it.

Angela had reprinted it as a large-scale canvas. The four levels – Individual, Team, Leadership, Organization – formed the backbone of the design. But this time, underneath each ring, they'd added a set of sticky notes mapping the Five Pillars to each level.

It wasn't just a framework anymore. It was an organizational map.

Sarah turned to the group.

'We've talked about where people feel meaning – now let's explore whether our environment is helping or hurting it.'

Each table was given one ecosystem level and asked to answer three questions:

1. Which of the Five Pillars are currently activated at this level?

2. Where are we unintentionally eroding meaning?

3. What are our quick wins – and what needs systemic change?

Insights started flowing fast:

- At the Individual level, teams noticed that values alignment was rarely discussed during onboarding. Even high-potential employees were unclear how their strengths linked to company priorities (Dik, Byrne and Steger, 2013; Park and Peterson, 2008).

- At the Team level, the pillar of Connection was patchy. In some teams, rituals like retros and learning moments were thriving. In others, psychological safety had been eroded by pressure and silence (Edmondson and Lei, 2014).

- The Leadership layer revealed blind spots in development and recognition. Mastery was expected – but rarely celebrated. And when under pressure, leaders reverted to control rather than coaching (Ulrich and Ulrich, 2010).

- Organizational systems were the slowest to shift. Promotions still favoured output over contribution. Strategy cycles prioritized efficiency over alignment. Resource allocation often bypassed feedback from those closest to the customer (Beer et al., 2016).

Angela summarized it clearly: 'You've been investing in engagement outcomes – but not the systems that create them.' She emphasized that Meaning Metrics don't replace engagement surveys – they deepen them. 'Engagement tells you if people are performing. Meaning tells you why.'

Sarah nodded, seeing it laid out in front of her. 'We have the data,' she said. 'But we haven't had the design.'

The team decided to begin an Ecosystem audit – a lightweight diagnostic process that used their own data, interviews and team reflections to track:

- How each pillar was experienced at each level

- Which Meaning Metrics were most or least activated

- Where systems, rituals and behaviours were aligned or in conflict

Sarah assigned every executive leader one level of the Ecosystem to sponsor.

'This isn't just a culture initiative,' she said. 'This is how we rebuild our performance system – around what actually drives it.'

Sustaining the ecosystem – from leadership to legacy

A month later, Sarah sat with Angela in the leadership development suite reviewing results from the organization's first Ecosystem audit.

The findings were clear – and humbling.

There were bright spots everywhere: one team had redesigned its learning rhythms to support Mastery; another had rebuilt its onboarding sequence around values alignment. A senior product leader had embedded 'impact conversations' into team retros, linking daily work to outcomes and clients.

But the gaps were clear too.

Recognition systems were still anchored in volume, not value. Strategic decision-making didn't yet include employee voice. Leadership behaviours varied too widely for meaning to be scalable.

'We're making progress,' Sarah said. 'But we still depend too much on individual leaders. Not enough is embedded into how the business runs.'

Angela nodded. 'You've done the diagnostic work,' she said. 'Now it's about systemic sustainability. Legacy leadership isn't what you build alone – it's what holds when you're not in the room.'

Together, they mapped out five meaning integration points – essential leverage areas for sustaining the ecosystem beyond individual programmes:

1. Business rhythm – how meaning shows up in quarterly planning, team check-ins and board reviews

2. People systems – how hiring, learning, performance and reward reinforce the Five Pillars

3. Leadership capability – whether your leaders are trained and expected to design for meaning

4. Cultural storytelling – which narratives are elevated, shared and celebrated

5. Governance and measurement – how Meaning Metrics are tracked and acted on at every level

Angela referenced a chapter from The Oxford Handbook of Positive Organizational Scholarship (Cameron and Spreitzer, 2012), which emphasized the role of system-wide design in embedding wellbeing and meaning into the infrastructure of organizations.

Sarah underlined the phrase in her notes: *Infrastructure for meaning.*

'That's our task now,' she said. 'To make meaning part of the business model – not just the employee experience.'

She remembered one of her early calls with Angela, before all of this began:

'If purpose is your signal,' Angela had said, 'then the Ecosystem is your amplifier.'

Meaning wasn't a project anymore. It was a system. A strategy. A legacy.

Final Reflection

Sarah closed the Meaning Lab session, then lingered behind while her team packed up their materials and headed for the lifts. The large canvas of the Ecosystem was still pinned to the wall, now covered in layers of insights, commitments and design ideas.

She stood quietly, taking it in.

This wasn't just a culture map anymore. It was an operating system for the kind of organization she wanted to build – and the kind of leader she wanted to be.

The breakthroughs from the Five Pillars were still resonating. But what this chapter had taught her was something deeper: that meaning wasn't just something individuals felt. It was something systems could cultivate – or suppress.

And it was her job, now, to ensure the design held. Not by controlling it, but by stewarding it. She thought back to something Angela had said early in their work together: 'If you want meaning to survive scale, it has to survive stress.'

The Ecosystem made that possible. Because when it's designed well, meaning doesn't rely on charisma. It relies on consistency.

Sarah paused for a moment before packing up. The journey they'd taken – from insight to behaviour to system – reminded her of something Angela had once shared: 'True transformation happens not when we push harder, but when we listen deeper.'

Angela had drawn from Otto Scharmer's Theory U which described the deeper arc of meaningful change: sensing what's really going on, 'presencing' a more conscious future and realizing it through aligned action.

The structures were in place. Awareness had deepened. But even the best-designed ecosystem needs activation. That activation comes from leaders through consistent everyday leadership behaviour.

In the next chapter, we turn to the human element: how leaders can lead with meaning using a simple, powerful playbook.

Takeaways

- Meaning must be embedded at multiple levels to be sustained. The Meaningful Work Ecosystem provides a multi-level model for designing meaning into the individual, team, leadership and organizational layers (Bronfenbrenner, 1977; Rosso et al., 2010).

- Personal experience of meaning is shaped by structural conditions. Employees don't work in isolation. Their sense of autonomy, mastery, connection, purpose and impact is directly affected by leadership behaviour, team norms and cultural systems (Edmondson and Lei, 2014; Bailey and Madden, 2016).

- The Five Pillars and Meaning Metrics become sustainable when supported by system design. Autonomy, Mastery, Purpose, Connection and Impact must be reinforced at every level through rituals, feedback, development and systems (Ulrich and Ulrich, 2010; Beer et al., 2016).

- Meaningful work is not just about people – it's about process. Most culture initiatives fail because they rely on inspiration and overlook alignment. Sustainable meaning requires systemic integrity (Thompson and Bunderson, 2003; Cameron and Spreitzer, 2012).

- The ecosystem is the amplifier. Purpose may be the signal – but it's the surrounding ecosystem that determines whether that signal is sustained, felt and activated over time.

Reflection Questions

1. Which level of your organization's ecosystem is currently most aligned with the Five Pillars – and which level is most at risk?

2. Are your managers and team leads supported to design for meaning – or are they expected to deliver outcomes without infrastructure?

3. How clearly are your people systems (e.g., performance, learning, recognition) reinforcing or eroding the experience of autonomy, mastery, purpose, connection and impact?

4. If you were to audit your organization's culture today, where would meaning be held by chance – and where would it be held by design?

5. What's the first step you could take to align your leadership behaviours, systems and stories around meaning as a strategic asset?

Chapter 7
Lead with meaning – a CEO's playbook

'I've learned that people will forget what you said,
people will forget what you did, but people will never
forget how you made them feel.'
Maya Angelou

Summary

This chapter introduces the practical heart of this book: how leaders behave when they are building meaningful cultures.

Sarah and her team have done the strategic work – identifying the Five Pillars of Meaningful Work, piloting Meaning Metrics and mapping the Meaningful Work Ecosystem across the business. Now comes the question every leader asks next: *What exactly should I be doing to lead this?*

We introduce the Lead with Meaning playbook – a behavioural model designed to help leaders activate meaning consistently and credibly at every level. It is not a leadership style. It is a set of observable practices and repeatable rituals through defined anchors that bring the Five Pillars to life in the day-to-day work of individuals and teams.

Each behaviour in the Lead with Meaning playbook aligns directly with the broader Meaning Over Purpose blueprint. It provides a simple, actionable answer to the question: *How do we close the Purpose-to-Meaning Gap – not once, but every day?*

This chapter also reflects the DNA of the Lead with Meaning Leadership Series – the programme now being rolled out across NexusNova. The series equips executives, directors and managers to lead meaningful teams by design, not by chance. The Lead with Meaning playbook they use is what you're about to learn.

For Sarah, this becomes the leadership pivot she's been searching for – a way to lead with trust, not control. With design, not wishful thinking. And with clarity, not charisma.

Because when leaders learn to lead with meaning, culture becomes strategy.

And performance becomes sustainable.

Leadership has changed – but our behaviours have not

Sarah flipped through one of her old leadership notebooks – a relic from the early days of her career.

She scanned the phrases: Set clear targets. Stay strong under pressure. Control the narrative. Maintain professional distance.

The handwriting was neater than she remembered. The tone was… sharper.

'This is what I was taught,' she thought. 'And what I learned to reward.'

None of it was wrong. But all of it was incomplete. Back then, the role of the leader was to protect, project and perform. You had to have answers. You had to hold the room. You had to deliver results – even if it came at the cost of transparency or trust.

It had worked. Until it didn't.

The world had changed.

Hybrid work had redefined connection. Employees expected more voice, more purpose and more growth. Burnout wasn't a badge of honour anymore – it was a warning sign. Generational shifts had moved the centre of gravity in culture from control to clarity, from output to meaning.

But leadership behaviours hadn't always caught up.

Sarah realized that the Five Pillars might be designed into the system – and that Meaning Metrics were being tracked – but without visible, consistent leadership behaviours to bring them to life, meaning would remain aspirational.

Angela had named it during a recent leadership session:

'Most senior leaders are trying to lead a new deal using old deal behaviours.'

The room had been quiet.

Sarah could see it clearly now. They'd evolved their values. They'd redesigned systems. They'd even introduced the Five Pillars. But in moments of pressure, leaders defaulted back to the habits they'd inherited: directive updates, binary ratings, shallow feedback loops, emotional distance dressed up as professionalism.

And that's where meaning got lost. Not in the strategy. In the behaviours. Angela had shared research from Kahn (1992) and Edmondson (2014) showing that people's sense of meaning and psychological presence at work is directly shaped by leadership behaviour – especially in how leaders handle risk, emotion and uncertainty. Cameron and Spreitzer (2012) confirmed this in system-wide studies: even in high-performing cultures, when leaders don't model meaning, it doesn't stick.

'If you want a meaningful culture,' Angela had said, 'you have to build meaningful leaders.' That, Sarah realized, was now the work. Not a new style. But a new leadership standard.

'That's where the Lead with Meaning playbook comes in,' Angela said. 'This isn't a new leadership style. It's a set of consistent, observable behaviours – the behavioural muscle that activates the system you've built.'

The Lead with Meaning playbook

The following week, Sarah stood in front of 30 NexusNova managers, preparing to open the first session of their new leadership programme.

This was the pilot of the Lead with Meaning Leadership Series – the practical companion to the strategic frameworks Sarah and her team had already implemented.

Angela was co-facilitating the session. She stepped to the front, opened her notebook and began with a single question:

'What does it feel like to be led by you?'

The room went still.

Angela let the silence hold.

'Not what do you *intend* or what do you *value* – but what do people actually experience when they work with you?'

Sarah glanced around the room. Many of these leaders were high performers. Smart. Kind. Committed. But few had ever been asked to lead through the lens of meaning.

Angela paused.

'This Lead with Meaning playbook is new language. But it stands on the shoulders of what great leadership has always been.'

Angela gestured to the flipchart behind her, where five leadership voices were listed:

- Robert Greenleaf – servant leadership: leadership begins by helping others grow (Greenleaf, 1977)

- Bill George – authentic leadership: show up with purpose, integrity and self-awareness (George, 2003)

- Jim Collins – Level 5 leadership: humble, disciplined builders outperform charismatic figureheads (Collins, 2005)

- Kim Cameron – positive leadership: gratitude, trust and amplification drive resilience and results (Cameron and Spreitzer, 2012)

- Margaret Wheatley – leadership in complexity: from hero to host (Wheatley, 2011)

'We're not here to be heroes anymore,' Angela said. 'We're here to be hosts. The ones who create the conditions for meaning to emerge.'

Sarah felt something shift in the room.

The Lead with Meaning playbook wasn't a reinvention. It was a distillation – a way to activate decades of insight into everyday practice.

'We've talked about the Five Pillars,' Angela said, 'and we've mapped the ecosystem. Now we focus on what you can influence most, every single day: your behaviour.'

She flipped the page to reveal the Lead with Meaning playbook – five repeatable behaviours designed to activate meaning in practice.

The five daily behaviours of meaning-driven leaders

Angela stepped forward, marker in hand.

'Before we get into tools and timelines,' she said, 'we need to talk about behaviours – the small things that make culture real.'

She wrote five words across the board:

Model. Translate. Coach. Connect. Celebrate.

'These are the daily repeatable practices of meaning-driven leadership,' she said. 'They don't require new systems or budget. They require intention. They activate the Five Pillars and turn intent into daily impact.'

Angela explained the practices, speaking as she wrote:

'Model – start with you. Be visible in your values, especially under pressure.

Translate – make purpose personal. Help people see why their work matters.

Coach – grow your people, not just your pipeline. Help them stretch, without snapping.

Connect – lead with trust and humanity. Make space for psychological safety.

Celebrate – reinforce what matters. Recognize not just outcomes, but effort and growth.'

Sarah leaned forward slightly. The room went still.

Angela smiled. 'You don't need to be a perfect leader. You need to be a present one. Let me explain what that looks like.'

Figure 11 highlights the core five behaviours of the Lead with Meaning playbook – a repeatable cycle of behaviours that bring the Five Pillars and Meaning Metrics to life.

Figure 11: The Lead with Meaning playbook outlines five repeatable leadership behaviours – Model, Translate, Coach, Connect and Celebrate – that activate meaningful work across all levels. These behaviours are reinforcing and cyclical, not sequential. When consistently practised, they embed meaning into daily leadership.

Model – start with you

Sarah thought of the moment two months earlier when she'd owned a strategic misstep in front of the board. Something had told her to show up with honesty.

'Model,' Angela said, 'isn't about having all the answers. It's about being visible in your values, especially when it's hard. People don't believe in meaning if they don't see you living it.'

A few leaders around the table nodded. This wasn't theory. It was how they showed up when the stakes were real.

Translate – make purpose personal

Angela drew a simple arrow between two words: vision → value.

'Purpose often lives in strategy decks,' she said. 'But meaning lives in daily work.'

Sarah felt a jolt of clarity. That's what we've been missing.

'Your job,' Angela continued, 'is to connect the dots, to help your people see how what they do today creates the future we've committed to. If you don't make that connection, no one else will.'

Coach – grow your people, not just your pipeline

Angela offered a challenge. 'This week, give someone feedback that helps them grow, not just perform.'

Sarah thought of Emilie, her strategy lead. Brilliant, capable but under-stretched. She realized she'd been managing Emilie's output, not her development.

'Coaching doesn't need to be formal,' Angela added. 'It's what happens in the moments you choose to invest with belief, stretch assignments and questions that unlock insight.'

Sarah underlined: *Stretch, not save.*

Connect – lead with trust and humanity

Angela looked around. 'When was the last time you asked your team, not just "how's the project?" but "how are you?"'

A ripple of recognition moved through the group.

'Connection fuels commitment,' she said. 'People do their best work when they feel seen, safe and valued.'

Sarah made a note to revisit her weekly 1:1s to make space for check-ins, not just task reviews.

Celebrate – reinforce what matters

Angela held up a Post-it®, something a junior team member had once left on her desk after a keynote: *You helped me remember why I started.*

'Recognition doesn't have to be grand,' she said. 'But it has to be real. Celebrate courage. Celebrate progress. Celebrate how people show up, not just what they deliver.'

Sarah thought back to a recent product launch. She'd thanked the team for the outcome, but hadn't paused to acknowledge the late nights, the problem-solving, the quiet persistence. *Celebrate the how,* she wrote, *not just the what.*

Angela stepped back from the board.

'These five behaviours aren't leadership theory,' she said. 'They're culture in action. They're how you embed meaning with presence.'

Sarah looked at the words again. They were deceptively simple. But she knew, if done consistently, they could change everything.

'We've focused so much on performance,' she said to her team. 'But maybe this is what unlocks it… meaning in motion.'

Angela nodded.

'This is what it means to be a meaning-driven leader. It's not about style. It's about consistency. Each of these habits activates the Five Pillars and reinforces the Meaning Metrics. They provide the human layer, the daily behaviours, that bridge strategy and experience.'

And the best way to test a playbook… is to play.

At NexusNova, Sarah and her leadership team began embedding these behaviours into real moments of connection, accountability and celebration.

Over the following weeks, Sarah began applying each habit, not as theory, but as practice. She shared a mistake openly with her board to demonstrate Model. She revised team briefs to begin with Translate, connecting every project back to purpose.

She had a meeting with Chey to brief and support him through a stretch project she'd previously hesitated on, an act of Coach. She deepened her 1:1s with Connect prompts that focused on how people were feeling, not just what they were doing.

And she introduced a ritual at the end of each all-hands, to Celebrate the impact people created, not just what they completed.

Sarah saw that the results of this didn't just shift the energy in the room. They were shaping the culture in motion.

The five anchors of meaning-driven leaders

Angela turned to the group.

'So how do these behaviours land?' she asked. 'How do people experience them?'

She wrote five phrases on the flipchart:

Show what matters through your actions

Frame the work with 'why'

Fuel progress and growth

Create connection and safety

Show the difference it makes

'These are your anchors,' she said. 'They're not extra steps. They are the emotional foundations that make leadership meaningful. They are how people *feel* when you lead this way.'

She walked across the room and pointed to the five behaviours still written on the whiteboard.

'Each anchor amplifies the power of a behaviour,' she continued. '*Translate* becomes deeply personal when you frame with "why". *Coach* fuels growth when you focus on small wins. *Connect* creates safety when you build belonging. *Celebrate* drives commitment when people see their impact. The anchors turn behaviour into belief.'

Sarah nodded slowly. The anchors were the bridge between doing and being. They ensured that the five behaviours weren't just visible — but *felt*.

Angela moved to the next page and began walking through each anchor, pausing to check for reflection as she spoke.

1. Show what matters through your actions

Pillars: Alignment

Metrics: Alignment, Resonance

Being a meaning-driven leader isn't about having all the answers. It's about being visible in your values, especially when it's hard. People don't believe in meaning if they don't see you taking actions that show you are living it.

This is the heart of leadership: living the values you stand for. In times of ambiguity, pressure, or change, people look to you, consciously or not, or evidence of what really matters here.

When you role model inclusion, accountability, care, or clarity, you build belief and signal direction. When your actions match your words, you create alignment. When they don't, people feel it, even if they can't always name it.

To show what matters means embodying what you expect from others. Not performatively, but consistently, and with integrity. When leaders do this, they become a source of trust and direction.

Angela looked down at her notebook to find a quote she wanted to share and said 'Kouzes and Posner's research found "Credibility is the foundation of leadership. If people don't believe in the messenger, they won't believe the message."'

Angela looked up 'this reminds us that modelling is one of the most powerful enablers of followership and credibility' (Kouzes and Posner, 2017).

Sarah had started to notice more often the micro-moments where values either lived or evaporated. She made a concerted effort to change how she showed up. Instead of telling her team that inclusion mattered, she made space for every voice in the room, even if it meant slowing the agenda.

She took the time in 1:1s and leadership meetings to openly name where she felt she had some blind spots and ask for feedback. And when tensions ran high during the merger discussions, she didn't default to control, she modelled transparency, sharing what she knew and what she didn't.

It wasn't dramatic. It was deliberate. Her team noticed. Trust deepened. People began speaking more honestly, not because they had been told to, but because they had seen it done.

2. Frame the work with 'why'

Pillars: Purpose, Impact

Metrics: Alignment, Resonance

Meaning-driven leaders don't just set goals – they give context. They connect the dots between what someone is doing and why it matters, both to the organization and to them personally. They link tasks to outcomes and connect individual contribution to team or organizational purpose.

Sarah had already begun trialling this in her exec team meetings – opening with 'why', not 'what'. The energy was different. People leaned in. They felt their work had weight.

This anchor draws on Wrzesniewski et al. (1997) and Grant (2007) – showing that when people understand the significance of their contribution, performance and commitment rise. It also echoes Sinek's (2014) call to 'Start with Why' – because when people know the reason behind the task, their energy shifts.

'Meaning doesn't need a manifesto,' Angela had said. 'It needs a sentence that connects "what I do" to "who it helps". This anchor is essential for activating the pillars of Purpose and Impact and it directly supports the Alignment and Resonance domains of the Meaning Metrics.'

3. Fuel progress and growth

Pillars: Mastery, Autonomy

Metrics: Growth, Resonance

This anchor is about recognizing and enabling progress – not just in results, but in people. Meaning-driven leaders create space for learning. They stretch without breaking. They ask growth-based questions in 1:1s. They give feedback focused on improvement, not compliance.

Angela referenced Csikszentmihalyi's (1990) theory of flow and Amabile and Kramer's (2011) *The Progress Principle*, both of which reinforce that small, visible wins can dramatically enhance engagement and meaning. This also links to Kouzes and Posner's (2017) practice of 'Enable Others to Act' – showing that empowering others builds ownership, trust and commitment.

She looked around the room. 'This is how you build capacity, not dependency.'

This behaviour reinforces the pillars of Mastery and Autonomy and strengthens Growth and Resonance – the motivational engines of resilience and long-term contribution.

4. Create connection and safety

Pillars: Connection, Mastery

Metrics: Connection, Growth

Angela took a breath. 'Let's talk about safety. Because meaning can't thrive without it.'

Meaning-driven leaders don't just build teams. They build trust. This anchor focuses on inclusion, psychological safety and relational leadership. Leaders show vulnerability. They model humanity. They ask people how they're doing – and make space to hear the answer.

Edmondson and Lei (2014) describe this as a learning culture, where people can take risks, speak their truth and feel they belong. Brown (2018) reinforces that vulnerability is not weakness – it is the foundation of connection. And Goleman's (1998) emotional intelligence model reminds us that self-awareness and empathy are essential for meaningful leadership.

Angela taught the group a micro-ritual:

> At the start of your next meeting, ask: 'What's one word for how you're arriving today?'

'This habit activates the Connection and Mastery pillars and strengthens psychological safety – which is core to the Meaning Metric of Connection.'

Sarah tried it. It took 30 seconds. And changed the room.

5. *Show the difference it makes*

Pillars: Impact, Purpose

Metrics: Impact, Resonance

Angela paused before speaking. 'The final habit is about closing the loop. Leaders make impact visible – through stories, feedback or data. They connect the dots between someone's effort and the difference it made.'

Sarah had trialled this by inviting frontline team members to monthly results meetings – not to be celebrated, but to *hear* how their work landed.

Angela cited Grant's (2007) research again – reminding the group that performance often increases when people can see the result of their contribution.

This anchor also reflects what Humphrey et al. (2015) described as 'meaning through emotional authenticity': when leaders name and share impact, people internalize their value more deeply. This in turn reinforces the pillar of Impact, the Meaning Metric of Resonance and ensures employees see and feel the outcomes of their work – a key to grit and long-term commitment.

Angela stepped back and paused she scanned the room to catch the eye of every leader. 'These five anchors are your meaning-makers, the emotional glue that transforms consistency into connection. They turn leadership from routine into resonance. When paired with each of the five behaviours, they create the full rhythm of meaningful leadership.'

As the session closed, Sarah watched the group reflect on the five anchors. No jargon. No big slogans. Just clear, grounded practices that – when done consistently – became culture in motion.

That was the full Lead with Meaning playbook. Not rules. Not roles. But repeatable leadership behaviours underpinned with anchors that close the Purpose-to-Meaning Gap one moment at a time.

From moments to culture – how habits scale meaning

Two weeks into the pilot, Sarah called a check-in with the first cohort of managers enrolled in the Lead with Meaning Leadership Series.

The energy was different now.

Leaders who had entered the programme feeling cautious were now animated, reflective, curious. They weren't just learning – they were reframing how they led.

'It's not about being a different person,' one team lead said. 'It's about showing up on purpose.'

Another added: 'These five anchors are starting to show up in how we talk. And in how people respond.'

Sarah smiled. That was the goal. Not a leadership revolution – but a shift in rhythm. From isolated effort to culture in motion.

Angela joined the session to show how these leadership anchors could now be integrated into the Ecosystem – reinforcing meaning at the individual, team, leadership and organizational levels.

'Now that we've explored the anchors,' she said, 'we need to think about how to scale them – through three powerful levers: language, rhythm and leadership modelling.'

She drew a simple diagram linking the Lead with Meaning playbook to the broader Meaningful Work Ecosystem:

- At the Individual level, the behaviours and anchors drive motivation and connection to role.

- At the Team level, they shape rituals, check-ins and norms.

- At the Leadership level, they model culture through behaviour.

- At the Organizational level, they inform how leaders are developed, evaluated and recognized.

'This is how behaviours become culture,' Angela said. 'Through consistency.'

This alignment ensured the Lead with Meaning playbook wasn't a separate initiative – but a human-powered thread woven through the entire ecosystem.

Embedding the habits through business rhythm

The team decided to start small by aligning the playbook with existing leadership moments:

- Monthly manager forums would now open with reflections on which behaviour had shaped performance that month.

- Performance conversations would include prompts like:
  - 'Where did you help someone connect to purpose?'
  - 'Where did you make progress visible?'

- Leadership development was updated to include the Lead with Meaning playbook as a core competency framework.

- A simple peer recognition tag – #MeaningInAction – was introduced on internal comms, celebrating leaders who practised the behaviours in real time.

Angela reminded the team of the research. The power of the Lead with Meaning playbook wasn't in perfection. It was in repetition. When leaders repeated these small, meaningful behaviours – even imperfectly – the culture learned to trust them.

'Habits scale meaning not through intensity, but through iteration,' she said. Leaders didn't need to be perfect. They needed to be intentional.

Sarah underlined one sentence on her tablet: *This is how we lead the system – not just the team.*

And in that moment, the Lead with Meaning playbook stopped being a pilot. It became the standard.

Final Reflection

As the final cohort session closed, Sarah stayed behind in the quiet room, the smell of coffee lingering and flipcharts still leaning against the wall. She glanced again at the board, where two lists were still visible.

The five behaviours:

Model. Translate. Coach. Connect. Celebrate.

And the five anchors:

Show what matters through your actions

Frame the work with 'why'

Fuel progress and growth

Create connection and safety

Show the difference it makes

Sarah saw these together as a rhythm. Behaviours that gave shape to leadership, and anchors that gave it depth.

It was deceptively simple. But she now knew this wasn't a tactical toolkit. It was a blueprint for how leaders could build trust, meaning and resilience, at scale.

Angela had described it not as a leadership style, but as a shift – from managing output to leading meaningfully.

From controlling to cultivating.

From performing to partnering.

From heroic expert to humble host.

Sarah had begun to see herself differently too – no longer as the person who had to carry culture alone, but as someone now capable of activating it through others. It reminded her of the models that Angela had shared throughout the programme:

- Greenleaf's servant leadership – about lifting others (Greenleaf, 1977)
- Bill George's authentic leadership – about values in action (George, 2003)
- Margaret Wheatley's 'Hero to Host' – about convening, not commanding (Wheatley, 2011)
- Collins's Level 5 leadership – about pairing humility with fierce resolve (Collins, 2005)

'We've had the theory for years,' Sarah thought. 'Now we finally have the practice.'

The Lead with Meaning playbook had become the practical expression of all they had built – a way to live the Five Pillars, sustain the Ecosystem and to make culture visible through daily acts of leadership.

And that, she realized, was how meaning moves – not through vision statements or strategies – but through leaders who lead differently.

You might be wondering, how would we know it's working? When leaders shift behaviour, we often feel the difference in meetings, in energy, in morale. But to sustain that shift, we need to track it.

In the next chapter, we introduce Meaning Metrics the four indicators that reveal whether your culture is building meaning or eroding it.

Takeaways

- Great leadership is meaning-led. The best leaders create environments of purpose, trust and contribution – not just delivery. The Lead with Meaning playbook operationalizes decades of leadership insight into daily practice (Greenleaf, 1977; George, 2003; Collins, 2005).

- The Lead with Meaning playbook builds on the Five Pillars of Meaningful Work, Meaning Metrics and Meaningful Work Ecosystem. It provides the behavioural muscle to activate meaning across leadership layers and within culture infrastructure – consistently and credibly.

- The five behaviours and five anchors work in tandem where doing and feeling are fully integrated. The behaviours provide the consistency and the anchors provide the resonance. Each element of the playbook connects to proven leadership principles and is validated by leadership science.

- This is the shift from inspiration to embodiment. Meaningful cultures aren't built by charismatic champions. They're built by consistent leaders who understand that their behaviour is the blueprint and that meaning is lived through action, not just intention.

- Lead with Meaning is not a leadership theory. It's a leadership standard. And it's how organizations move from purpose to performance – through people.

Reflection Questions

1. Which of the five behaviours and five anchors do you naturally model – and which do you avoid, consciously or not?

2. In times of pressure, which behaviour or anchor do you tend to drop first – and what would it take to keep it present?

3. How does your current leadership style align with the evolution from 'hero' to 'host' – and what might need to shift?

4. What small ritual or behaviour could you begin using tomorrow to build more meaning into how you lead?

5. What would it take to embed the Lead with Meaning playbook as a leadership standard – not just in your own leadership but as the cultural leadership norm in your organization?

Chapter 8
Meaning Metrics – a new dashboard for culture and performance

'What gets measured gets managed.'
Peter Drucker

Summary

This chapter introduces the next evolution of the Meaning Over Purpose blueprint – a model for measuring what matters most.

Sarah and her team had begun to design meaning into the employee experience. But now came the harder question: *How do you know if it's working?*

For decades, organizations have measured culture through lagging indicators – engagement scores, retention rates, exit interviews. But these only tell part of the story and often too late. If leaders are serious about embedding meaning into their ecosystem, they need a way to track it in real time before the culture unravels.

We introduce Meaning Metrics, a practical, research-informed framework that measures the leading indicators of meaningful work: Alignment, Growth, Connection and Resonance. Each metric is grounded in decades of academic literature. We also explore how Meaning Metrics can be integrated into strategy dashboards, linking culture to financial performance through a modernized version of the balanced scorecard. Through treating meaning as a measurable business system, leaders create cultural resilience, not just cultural rhetoric.

For Sarah and her team, Meaning Metrics become more than a diagnostic. They become the dashboard for designing a culture that performs.

Why traditional metrics fall short – and what leaders really need

Sarah stared at the culture dashboard for Q2. The graphs looked… fine.

Engagement had ticked up slightly. Retention was steady. Pulse survey participation was up. But something wasn't sitting right.

She remembered the tension in last week's team debrief – the visible fatigue on her top product lead, the flat responses during a major client pitch. None of it was reflected in the numbers.

'How do we still have decent scores,' she thought, 'when we're this tired?'

Angela had said it early in their work together:

'Most culture dashboards track symptoms – not causes. Engagement is the outcome. Meaning is the input.'

Sarah pulled out a printed copy of the company's last engagement report. It used a familiar format – a modified version of Gallup's Q12. She scanned the items:

- 'I know what is expected of me at work.'
- 'I have a best friend at work.'
- 'My manager seems to care about me as a person.'
- 'The mission of my company makes me feel my job is important.'

'These are valid engagement indicators,' Angela had explained, 'but they don't tell you if people feel meaning – if they're aligned, growing, connected or energized. That's what we need to track.'

Angela had introduced her to the work of Steger, Dik and Duffy (2012), specifically the WAMI scale, which asked sharper, deeper questions:

- 'I understand how my work contributes to my life's meaning.'
- 'I view my work as contributing to the greater good.'
- 'I find personal fulfilment in my role.'

'Now that,' Sarah thought, 'is what I need to know.'

The WAMI was one example. Angela had also shown her validated insights from Saks (2006) on the drivers of job engagement, Fisher (2010) on wellbeing at work and McKee (2014) on the emotional tone of cultures.

All pointed to the same truth: most current metrics tracked sentiment; fewer tracked meaning. That's when Angela built a framework to augment the work of others and introduced the Meaning Metrics framework.

Not a replacement for engagement surveys. Not another benchmarking tool. But a new lens – one that measured the leading indicators of meaningful work.

Angela was clear:

'Meaning Metrics is our proprietary framework. It includes four core domains – Alignment, Growth, Connection and Resonance – and offers a diagnostic that helps you see where culture is building meaning… or eroding it.'

She went on to explain that while the framework was proprietary, the tools used to deliver it were flexible. Depending on the client, validated academic measures like WAMI, Gallup Q12 items or Deloitte's Employee Experience Index could be integrated.

Sarah liked that. It wasn't dogmatic. It was designed to meet the organization where it was.

'It's not just new language,' she'd told her team. 'It's a new dashboard.'

And one that measured what people were really asking for: not just *Are you engaged?*, but *Do you feel meaning in what you do – and in how we lead?*

Introducing the four core Meaning Metrics – what we measure and why

Angela stood up and walked to the whiteboard at the front of the room in the strategy session, marker in hand, and introduced the Meaning Metrics framework – a simple but powerful quadrant model.

'There are four things that determine whether someone feels their work is meaningful,' she said. 'Alignment, Growth, Connection and Resonance. If you want to close the Purpose-to-Meaning Gap, this is how you track whether your efforts are working.'

She paused, letting the group absorb the words. 'Each one tells us something specific about how people experience meaning in your organization. And together, they create a dashboard that shows where meaning is happening – and where it's being blocked.'

Sarah looked around the room. These weren't abstract ideas anymore. These were new indicators of organizational health and early signals if they are missing.

Angela began with the first quadrant.

1. Alignment – 'Do I connect with what this organization stands for?'

This domain measures the extent to which employees feel that their values, purpose and strengths are aligned with the company's mission and the role they play within it.

'When alignment is high,' Angela said, 'people experience congruence between their personal values and what the organization stands for. It strengthens Purpose, supports Autonomy and reinforces emotional commitment.'

'When this is low,' she continued, 'you get surface-level compliance. People show up. But they're not *in* it.'

Steger et al. (2012) call this 'meaningfulness in work' – the personal resonance and sense of congruence between one's role and oneself. Gallup's Q12 echoes this in the item: 'The mission or purpose of my company makes me feel my job is important.'

This domain is tightly linked to the Five Pillars of Purpose and Autonomy.

2. Growth – 'Am I learning, progressing and developing?'

Growth measures whether people believe they are learning, stretching and moving forward – not just in job title, but in skill, maturity and confidence.

Angela reminded the group that growth doesn't have to mean promotion. It means motion. 'Mastery is one of the strongest motivators we have,' she said, referencing Deci and Ryan's (2000) self-determination theory and Amabile and Kramer's (2011) work on progress as a primary driver of motivation.

Angela went on to caution that Saks (2006) found that development opportunities are among the strongest predictors of engagement, but only when paired with autonomy and feedback.

This metric reflects the Five Pillars of Mastery and Autonomy and connects to individual and team levels in the Ecosystem. When growth scores are low, meaning erodes quickly – even in high-performing cultures.

3. Connection – 'Do I feel seen, safe and part of something here?'

Connection goes beyond 'Do I like my team?' It asks whether people feel emotionally safe, respected and included; whether they feel they belong.

'This is where psychological safety lives,' Angela said, citing Edmondson and Lei (2014). 'And it's one of the strongest cultural predictors of innovation and resilience.'

Connection is the emotional infrastructure of the ecosystem. It underpins psychological safety, trust and belonging. Without it, the other metrics cannot hold. Research from SHRM/Globoforce (2018) confirms that cultures high in recognition, trust and emotional closeness have significantly lower attrition and higher discretionary effort.

This domain connects to the Five Pillars of Connection and Mastery and shows up across team and leadership levels in the ecosystem.

4. Resonance – 'Does my work energize me? Does it feel worthwhile?'

The final domain, Resonance, asks a more emotional, experiential question.

It reflects whether work feels worth doing – whether people experience pride, satisfaction or personal meaning in what they contribute. It's a synthesis metric. Resonance captures emotional energy – the felt experience of contribution, pride and purpose. It is the clearest signal of meaning at work.

Angela drew from Fisher's (2010) review on workplace happiness and the broader literature on emotional culture (McKee, 2014). She described Resonance as the feeling that your work connects back to you. 'It's about whether people feel a spark,' she said. 'Not every day. But often enough that they know it's still there.'

This metric connects to Impact, Purpose and Autonomy – and shows up strongly at the individual and leadership levels in the ecosystem.

Angela stepped back and pointed to the four words again.

'Together, these aren't just sentiment measures. They're strategic indicators of where meaning is working – and where culture needs to be redesigned.'

Sarah looked at the model. She didn't see a survey tool. She saw a new dashboard. One that finally made the intangible, visible.

How Meaning Metrics integrates with existing culture and business data

The day after their strategy session, Sarah joined a call with NexusNova's Head of People Analytics and CFO. The agenda was clear: how to integrate Meaning Metrics into the company's existing reporting suite.

'We're not looking to replace our systems,' Sarah explained. 'We're looking to enhance them – to measure what we *say* matters.'

Leonie had already done a rough map. The company's current dashboard included:

- Gallup Q12 results
- Monthly pulse scores (engagement, wellbeing)
- Quarterly attrition and exit trends
- Productivity and customer satisfaction metrics
- Internal mobility and promotion rates

'It's good data,' Angela said. 'But none of it tells you whether people feel meaning in the experience of work.'

She shared how other organizations were beginning to integrate meaning-based indicators into their scorecards – citing insights from Deloitte (2020), Microsoft Workplace Analytics (2021) and the Qualtrics XM Institute (2022). These companies weren't asking, *Are you happy at work?* They were asking, *Do you feel that what you do matters – to you and to us?* That shift made the data meaningful.

'This is the difference between tracking noise and tracking signals,' Angela explained.

Mapping Meaning Metrics to existing dashboards

See Figure 12, the Meaning Metrics framework, for the four leading indicators of culture and performance – Alignment, Growth, Connection and Resonance.

Angela showed how the four domains could fit within their current framework:

1. Alignment could be mapped to purpose engagement scores and onboarding feedback.

2. Growth aligned with learning hours, promotion rates and 1:1 frequency.

3. Connection correlated with psychological safety scores, peer recognition and social network analysis.

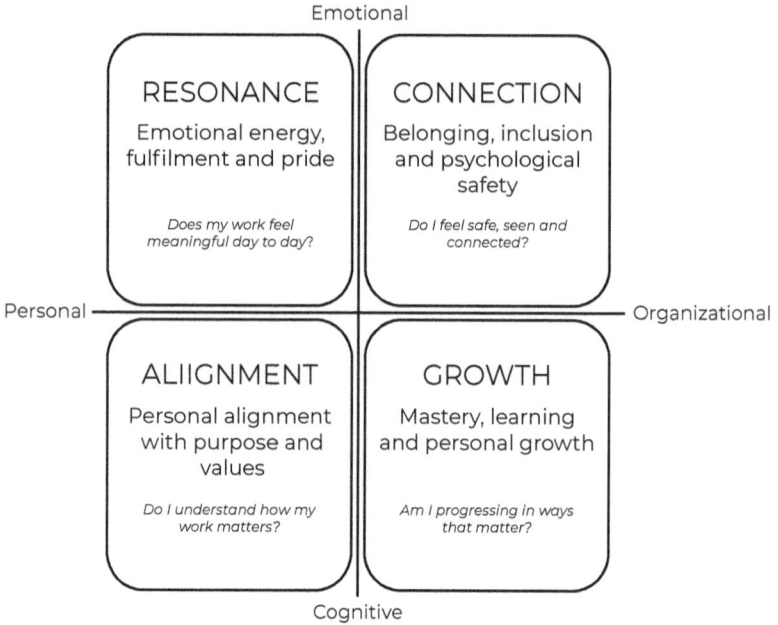

Figure 12: The Meaning Metrics framework introduces four leading indicators of meaningful work: Alignment, Growth, Connection and Resonance. Designed to sit alongside traditional KPIs, these metrics are modular, repeatable and focused on what matters most to people and business performance.

4. Resonance could be tracked through narrative feedback, exit interview themes and new pulse-style micro-check-ins (e.g., 'How energized did you feel at work this week?').

She cited Kaplan and Norton's Balanced Scorecard (1996) to make the case that culture and people metrics have always been part of strategic success under learning and growth. The problem wasn't only that people didn't value them over financial measures. It was that they hadn't known how to measure the right things.

Sarah underlined a single line: *Meaning Metrics are not sentiment measures. They're strategy indicators.*

Angela emphasized that the framework was designed to be modular. 'Some clients use it to enhance pulse surveys. Others integrate it into leadership scorecards, engagement dashboards or even strategy reviews.'

That's what made it powerful: it didn't fight existing systems; it just made them more relevant.

Sarah looked at the evolving dashboard on screen – meaning indicators beside performance KPIs, culture feedback layered into talent analytics. 'This,' she thought, 'is what it means to measure what matters.'

Building a culture dashboard that drives action

Sarah stood in the boardroom alongside Leonie and the Head of People Analytics. On the screen was the first prototype of their Meaning Metrics dashboard.

It didn't look like a typical HR report.

There were no RAG-rated scores, no colour-coded 'engagement' tiles. Instead, there were four core quadrants – Alignment, Growth, Connection, Resonance – each with its own set of pulse insights, narrative quotes and meaning-linked indicators.

Angela had helped them create the structure – a hybrid model that integrated internal data, selected WAMI questions (Steger et al., 2012) and new short-form pulse items developed from practitioner best practice. The metrics were simple, repeatable and actionable.

Meaning Metrics became the human side of their performance dashboard – the missing quadrant that explained why people stayed, tried, stretched or silently disengaged.

From data to decision

Under Alignment, they tracked:

- The percentage of employees who said their role aligned with personal values
- How often employees referenced purpose or mission in internal feedback
- Onboarding responses to 'I feel I can be myself here'

Under Growth, they tracked:

- Self-reported learning and development scores
- Career conversations held per quarter
- The percentage of managers using growth-focused 1:1 templates

Under Connection, they tracked:

- Team psychological safety (via Edmondson-style diagnostics)
- Recognition activity by team and function
- 'Relationship depth' in collaboration mapping (via Microsoft Workplace Analytics)

Under Resonance, they tracked:

- Net emotional energy score ('How energized did you feel at work this week?')
- The percentage of people who said their work 'felt worthwhile'
- Exit themes linked to purpose and fulfilment

Each metric was accompanied by a 'next conversation' recommendation – a behavioural cue for leaders.

'This isn't just a measurement tool,' Angela reminded them. 'It's a conversation engine.'

Aligning with business rhythm

They embedded the dashboard into three organizational routines:

1. Monthly leadership check-ins: used to discuss culture health alongside delivery metrics
2. Quarterly board reports: culture data visualized alongside financials
3. Manager development: Lead with Meaning playbook alignment tracked using Meaning Metrics feedback

The team used the dashboard to flag early warning signals, identify hot spots and – most importantly – to recognize where meaning was thriving.

'What gets measured gets managed,' Sarah said. 'But what gets managed with meaning gets momentum.'

Angela reminded them of a core principle: 'Dashboards don't change culture. Leaders acting on dashboards change culture.' That was the shift. And this was the tool that made it possible.

Sarah looked at the final screen. This wasn't a report. It was a map. A way to lead culture with the same clarity they used to lead performance.

And that, she realized, was what they'd been missing all along.

'When you track what matters to people,' Angela said, 'you make culture measurable. And when leaders act on that data, you make culture trustworthy.'

Final Reflection

As Sarah prepared for the quarterly board update, she opened the newly integrated culture dashboard.

It sat alongside customer NPS, product velocity and quarterly revenue.

Not below them. Beside them.

Each quadrant – Alignment, Growth, Connection, Resonance – had a clear data point, a pattern to explore and a defined leader action. But what struck Sarah most was what one of her managers had said earlier that week:

'It's not that we never cared about meaning. It's that we didn't know how to see it.'

Now they could.

Angela's voice came back to her. Culture data should be more than informative; it should be transformative: 'When you start measuring meaning, you're not softening your metrics. You're sharpening your focus on performance through people.'

And that, Sarah now realized, was how culture became not just a promise, but a practice. Now they didn't just say that culture mattered. They could prove it and lead with it. Meaning Metrics had done what traditional surveys couldn't: they showed what really mattered, to the people who made the business run.

With that, the blueprint was complete. They had identified the gaps. Defined the Five Pillars, the motivational core. Designed the Ecosystem, the structural scaffolding. Developed the Lead with Meaning playbook, the daily activation. And now, built the Meaning Metrics dashboard, a way to track and improve what mattered most.

In Part III, we turn to the final challenge: sustaining it. Scaling meaning across the enterprise. And ensuring the culture holds, not just for today, but for tomorrow's leaders too.

Takeaways

- You cannot lead what you don't measure. Meaningful work has been difficult to track because leaders have lacked a clear framework. Meaning Metrics fills that gap by providing actionable, research-backed domains that reflect how people experience meaning in their work (Steger et al., 2012; Saks, 2006; Fisher, 2010).

- The Meaning Metrics – Alignment, Growth, Connection and Resonance – are leading indicators of culture performance. They reflect not just whether people are engaged, but why. And they offer practical guidance to leaders on where meaning is being built or lost.

- The model is both proprietary and integrative. Meaning Metrics provides a standardized architecture, but it flexes to include external validated tools such as WAMI (Steger et al., 2012), Gallup Q12 (Gallup, 2019) or Deloitte's employee experience analytics (Deloitte, 2020), depending on organizational needs.

- Meaning Metrics align with business dashboards. Just as leaders track financials or customer outcomes, they can now track meaning – through short pulse check-ins, narrative feedback and clear design levers (Kaplan and Norton, 1996; Microsoft, 2021; SHRM/Globoforce, 2018).

- This is how purpose becomes performance. Meaning Metrics give leaders visibility into whether their culture is delivering what their strategy promises – and that, in today's world, is not optional. It's essential.

Reflection Questions

1.   What are you currently measuring that tells you whether people feel meaning in their work – not just whether they are engaged?

2.   How would you assess each of the four Meaning Metrics – Alignment, Growth, Connection and Resonance – in your team or organization today?

3.   Where might your existing KPIs or dashboards be unintentionally hiding early warning signs of meaning erosion?

4.   What systems or rituals could you redesign to start capturing culture as you go, instead of retroactively?

5.   Who in your organization is best placed to help you design a Meaning Metrics dashboard – and what's the first step?

PART III

SCALING AND SUSTAINING MEANING – FUTURE-PROOFING ORGANIZATIONS

Sarah stepped into the boardroom with a quiet certainty. The walls bore no slogans. The team wore no matching lanyards. But something deeper had taken hold.

Leaders were using new language. Rituals had changed. Data dashboards now included culture as seriously as customer metrics. And when a junior engineer suggested a redesign of their onboarding experience to include storytelling and purpose – no one questioned it.

'It's happening,' Sarah thought. 'Not because I'm driving it. But because they believe in it.'

This is the moment every visionary CEO hopes for: when the culture begins to carry itself.

But what comes next is even more important. How do you keep that culture from drifting? How do you protect it – not from resistance, but from erosion?

And how do you make sure it not only survives growth, complexity and change – but thrives through it?

This concluding section of the book takes us from implementation to longevity. From culture activation to culture stewardship.

You'll see how Sarah – and now Zainab – begin to:

- Embed meaningful work into the fabric of organizational culture, strategy and structure.
- Lead through complexity, resistance and growth without losing the soul of the business.
- Design systems and succession models that protect values during change and scale.
- Build a legacy where meaningful work outlasts any one leader.

Angela introduces new frameworks here, including the Legacy Design Loop and deeper application of the Meaningful Work Ecosystem, to help leaders not only build but preserve what matters most.

Giovanni reappears, transformed from sceptic to steward. Zainab steps into her role as CEO, not to copy Sarah's vision, but to evolve it. And Sarah? She begins the final act of leadership: letting go – and watching it hold.

This is where meaningful work stops being a pilot.

It becomes a practice.

A philosophy.

A future.

Welcome to Part III – the moment where meaning moves from movement… to legacy.

Chapter 9
Embedding meaning – making culture your competitive advantage

'Culture eats strategy for breakfast.'
Peter Drucker

Summary

We now explore how meaning becomes a source of competitive advantage.

Sarah has introduced the Five Pillars, rolled out Meaning Metrics and begun training leaders through the Lead with Meaning playbook. But now comes the critical shift: moving from activation to embedment, from early traction to long-term transformation.

We show how organizations embed meaning into their culture using Angela's model of cultural integration through rhythm, systems and behaviour. This aligns with foundational research from Schein (2010) on how leaders shape culture through values, symbols and norms and with

Denison's (1990) findings that involvement, consistency and purpose are key cultural traits that drive long-term business effectiveness.

We also draw from Kotter and Heskett's (2008) work on culture and performance, Cameron et al. (2011) on positive practices and Chatman and O'Reilly (2016) on how strong cultures with aligned meaning foster agility and innovation. Case studies such as Zappos (Hsieh, 2010) and visionary companies like those in Built to Last (Collins and Porras, 1994) reinforce the idea that meaning-rich organizations are more likely to engage talent, build trust and outperform competitors.

For Sarah and her team, embedding meaning means aligning systems with story – reinforcing purpose through practices.

This chapter shows how to do exactly that – turning culture from rhetoric into a repeatable edge.

Beyond initiatives – why culture is what actually scales

The message came through late on a Friday.

Sarah saw it as she was clearing her inbox – a short email from Giovanni Mancini, CEO of LyriaTech.

> *Sarah – been following some of what you're doing. We've hit some walls.*
>
> *Would value a chat if you're open to it. No urgency – just curious. G.*

She stared at it for a moment.

Giovanni. The same CEO who, just a year ago at the Future of Work Summit, had dismissed culture as a 'nice-to-have'. The one who spoke about transformation only in terms of platforms, speed and operational agility. Smart. Strategic. Successful.

But now curious. And that told her everything.

Earlier that week, Sarah had been reflecting with Angela on the transformation NexusNova had begun. They were gaining traction.

The Five Pillars were understood. The Meaning Metrics were embedded. The Lead with Meaning playbook was in motion.

And yet, Angela had challenged her:

'Traction isn't the same as transformation. Culture only becomes a competitive advantage when it stops depending on momentum – and starts depending on design. Meaningful culture isn't a sprint. It's a system. And systems don't scale through pilot programmes. They scale through rhythm.'

Sarah had nodded. She was starting to feel it herself. The energy that followed a pilot. The enthusiasm after a training. The bump in survey scores.

But unless those moments were reinforced – repeatedly, across teams, rituals and time – they would evaporate under pressure.

Angela shared a quote from Schein (2010), one of the most influential voices in organizational culture:

> 'The only thing of real importance that leaders do is to create and manage culture.'

'Culture,' Angela said, 'is how your purpose survives pressure. And meaning is how people make sense of that purpose in their work. You've started creating it; now you have to embed it.'

That was the challenge ahead: not more initiatives, but a cultural infrastructure that embedded meaning through systems, rituals and daily decisions.

Sarah pulled out her notebook and wrote a single phrase:

What scales is culture.

She remembered one of her early beliefs – that strategy would be enough. That if she got the business model, customer value and execution right, everything else would follow.

But over time, she'd seen what the research confirmed:

- Strong cultures outperform weak ones, especially in uncertain times (Kotter and Heskett, 2008).

- Meaning-rich cultures increase resilience, agility and customer experience (Cameron et al., 2011).

- Culture is what people default to when no one is watching (Schein, 2010).

- Purpose and values embedded into norms, systems and symbols are what sustain performance (Denison, 1990; Collins and Porras, 1994).

Angela had a phrase Sarah had come to repeat often: *Culture is how meaning gets protected – not just when it's celebrated, but when it's tested.*

That was the shift Sarah was beginning to lead – and the one Giovanni was now noticing from the outside.

It wasn't about one more programme. It was about embedding meaning into the culture's DNA – through decisions, behaviours, symbols and design. To be able to scale without dilution.

And that's what they were about to do next.

From culture as intent to culture as infrastructure

Two days later, Sarah sat down with her executive team and the Culture and People leads to reflect on a deceptively simple question:

'What makes meaning hold – especially when things get hard?'

It wasn't a rhetorical discussion.

The company was entering another growth phase – new product lines, regional expansion, more pressure on delivery. And Sarah wanted to ensure that the cultural momentum they'd built didn't dissolve into well-intentioned posters and forgotten pilot programmes.

Angela had laid it out plainly: 'Culture isn't what you say. It's what gets reinforced when you're under pressure.'

Sarah nodded. That aligned with what she'd been seeing: when deadlines loomed, leaders reverted to task-first mode. Feedback shrank. Autonomy disappeared. Recognition got skipped. Not because people didn't care, but because the culture hadn't yet become infrastructure.

Angela outlined three simple truths:

1. Meaning scales through systems, not values.

2. Culture is projected through reinforcement, not purpose.

3. Behaviour is embedded through rituals, not strategy.

'And you already have the building blocks,' she reminded them. 'the Five Pillars are your emotional architecture. The Lead with Meaning playbook is your behavioural system. The Meaning Metrics are your dashboard. Now it's time to embed all three.

This, she explained, is why meaning must move from intent to infrastructure.

Sarah pulled up the Ecosystem – the four-level map that had helped her team connect personal experience, team rituals, leadership behaviour and organizational systems. Now it became the foundation for long-term embedding.

Angela walked the team through the structure again – with one core question:

'Where are we enabling the Five Pillars – and where are we eroding them through our systems?'

The goal wasn't scale through consistency. It was scale through congruence, where behaviours, systems and stories all told the same cultural truth. Sarah thought to herself that this was the question that all CEO's asked even if not out loud: *How do we scale meaning beyond a pilot, beyond a programme, beyond one inspiring leader?*

Angela then outlined the three core levers that convert culture from intention to infrastructure:

1. Rituals – *what people repeat without being told*

Rituals are small, visible acts that signal what matters. They don't live in handbooks – they live in calendars, in how meetings start, in what gets recognized.

'If you want to embed meaning,' Angela said, 'make it visible in what you repeat.' She cited Cameron et al. (2011) who found that positive workplace rituals – including recognition, storytelling and shared reflection – significantly increased engagement and innovation.

At NexusNova, the team began identifying their own anchor rituals:

- Kick-offs started with 'Why this matters'
- Stand-ups closed with 'Where did we feel progress?'
- Leadership check-ins asked, 'Who did we grow this week?' – not just 'What did we deliver?'

These were simple. But they scaled.

These rituals mapped directly to the Lead with Meaning playbook anchors: showcasing what matters, framing with why, showing progress through growth, creating safety and making impact visible. They weren't add-ons. They were meaning in motion.

2. Systems – *what gets tracked, rewarded and resourced*

Angela turned to Leonie who was partnering with Sarah on the culture change and asked 'How do your systems signal what you actually value?'

They all laughed – and nodded. Everyone knew that even the most inspiring culture could be undone by a performance system that rewarded outcomes without development or a promotion process that ignored leadership behaviours.

Angela referenced Denison (1990) and Schein (2010), who both stressed that culture is embedded when systems align with values – not contradict them. Kaplan and Norton's Balanced Scorecard (1996) was cited again as a model for integrating people metrics with strategy.

'If your systems reward delivery but ignore development or celebrate outcomes but minimize learning,' Angela said, 'then meaning erodes – even with the best intentions.'

Together, the team ran a Cultural Alignment Audit – mapping every major system to the Five Pillars – to see where meaning was being reinforced or contradicted, including:

- Performance reviews
- Bonus structures
- Talent processes
- Strategy offsites

3. Stories – *what gets told, remembered and passed on*

The final lever was storytelling.

'What do people repeat in the hallways? What gets shared at town halls? What are the origin myths?' asked Angela. She reminded the group of Collins and Porras (1994), who found that visionary companies didn't just have purpose – they had purpose with story.

Zappos was a classic example. As Hsieh (2010) described in *Delivering Happiness*, their 'wow' customer stories weren't just anecdotes – they were culture activation devices; a way to reinforce what mattered and why.

At NexusNova, Sarah asked every team to begin collecting 'meaning moments' – stories of where the Five Pillars showed up unexpectedly:

- A new hire taking initiative (Autonomy)

- A manager celebrating progress (Mastery)

- A team member feeling seen (Connection)

- A support rep learning how their resolution impacted a client's life (Impact)

Those stories didn't just inspire. They taught culture.

Figure 13 summarizes the three core levers that bring culture to life – and keep it embedded beyond posters or policies.

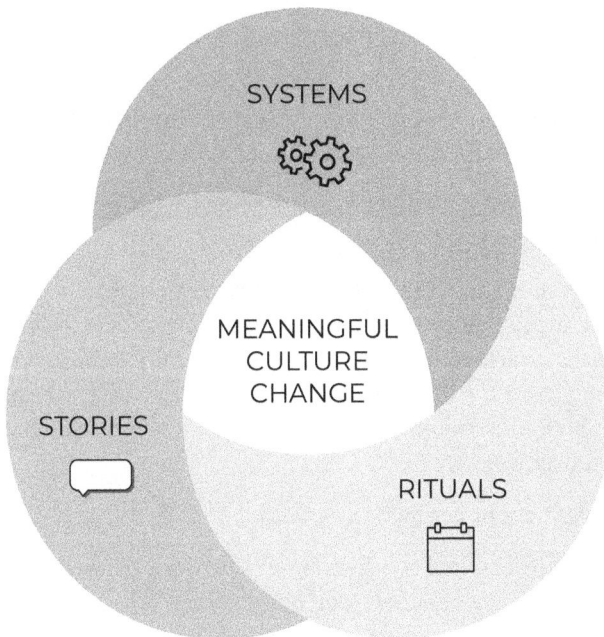

Figure 13: The Culture Carriers of Meaning – rituals, systems and stories – make values visible and scalable. They show what we celebrate, reinforce what we reward and embed what we believe. Together, they shape culture that is scalable, authentic and sustained.

Angela stood with Leonie by her side. 'This is how meaning embeds. Not through belief – through structure, rhythm and language.'

And Sarah realized something important. Culture wasn't what her team said. It was what they did – when no one was watching.

What gets protected gets passed on

Three months after the Meaning Metrics dashboard went live, Sarah supported by Leonie gathered her executive team for an offsite.

It wasn't about new strategy. It was about one question: *How do we protect what we've built – especially as we scale?*

They'd made enormous progress. The Five Pillars were embedded in team rituals. Managers were leading differently. Exit interviews now included questions about meaning, not just morale. And the new manager onboarding programme included a dedicated module on leading with meaning.

But they all knew what could happen next.

'The real test isn't if it works now,' Angela had warned. 'The real test is whether it holds during pressure. Or change. Or growth.'

That was what defined cultural integrity. Not what gets declared. But what gets protected.

Angela referenced Schein's (2010) cultural model again – noting that culture becomes real when leaders consistently model and reinforce desired behaviours, even when it's inconvenient. Denison (1990) and Kotter and Heskett (2008) made the same point: that the difference between high-performing cultures and the rest isn't intention. It's alignment over time.

Sarah thought about her own leadership.

When had she defaulted to old habits? When had pressure pulled her away from the behaviours she wanted to model?

'This is the pivot,' she said. 'From meaning as idea to meaning as integrity.'

Protecting meaning through leadership stewardship

With Leonie's guidance, the team created a simple list:

- Which rituals do we continue even when we're busy?

- Which stories do we retell when we onboard new teams?

- What behaviours get recognized – even when they're not attached to KPIs?

- Where are our systems quietly signalling something different?

They also identified their next phase of risks:

- Scaling across geographies

- Navigating the complexity of hybrid/hub-and-spoke working

- Retaining culture as new leaders and hires joined

- Holding the line on growth without burnout

Angela framed it clearly: 'Culture doesn't erode because leaders stop believing in it. It erodes because no one's assigned to protect it.'

This was the handover point from transformation to stewardship. From Sarah driving culture, to the system carrying it.

They formally activated the Culture Steward Network – a group of peer-nominated leaders trained to spot drift, tell stories, model the Lead with Meaning playbook and feed Meaning Metrics insights back into strategy.

Sarah also began hosting quarterly cultural retros – not just to celebrate meaning, but to audit where it was at risk. Each one opened with the same questions:

What's getting repeated? What's being forgotten? And what's the gap between what we say and what we signal?

Because what was protected, was passed on. And that, she now knew, was how meaning endured. (*Use Appendix 2: Meaningful Work Cultural Embedding Audit to stress-test your culture during periods of rapid growth or change.*)

Final Reflection

Sarah walked the floor of their newest regional hub, three months after the official launch. The space was modern, bright, efficient – everything she wanted it to be. But what made her smile wasn't the architecture.

It was what she overheard.

A frontline team leader was explaining to a new hire why the team always began their week with 'Where did we make a difference?' Another manager was prepping for a client meeting by asking 'Which pillar are we modelling here?'

There were no posters in sight. But the culture was loud.

The Five Pillars weren't being explained anymore. They were being lived.

The Lead with Meaning playbook wasn't in training decks. It was in team meetings.

Meaning Metrics weren't filed away in HR. They were on strategy dashboards.

'This is it,' Sarah thought. 'Not culture as promise – culture as practice.'

Meaning hadn't been achieved. It had been embedded. And that was how it would last.

But even with strong design, change brings resistance. Old habits resurface. New leaders may not buy in. And employees who've seen initiatives fade before might quietly hold back. Sarah understood now: embedding meaning wasn't just about systems; it was also about surfacing the barriers that stop them from sticking.

The next chapter explores how to lead through that resistance and sustain change when the culture starts to shift.

Takeaways

- Culture is how meaning becomes sustainable. It's not what leaders say – it's what gets reinforced, protected and passed on, especially under pressure (Schein, 2010; Denison, 1990).

- Embedding meaning means embedding systems. Meaning doesn't hold through inspiration alone. It is scaled through rituals, rhythms and structures that align with values (Kotter and Heskett, 2008; Cameron et al., 2011).

- Meaningful cultures outperform over time. Research shows that companies with strong cultural alignment – especially around purpose, belonging and shared meaning – have greater resilience, innovation and financial performance (Collins and Porras, 1994; Chatman and O'Reilly, 2016; Deloitte, 2016).

- Zappos and other purpose-led organizations prove the point. As Tony Hsieh showed, when culture is embedded through every interaction, it doesn't just retain talent – it attracts loyalty, customer trust and business growth (Hsieh, 2010).

- What gets protected, gets passed on. Meaning survives scale and change when leaders model it, systems reinforce it and culture stewards protect it. That's how meaning becomes legacy.

Reflection Questions

1. Where in your organization is culture still living as intent, rather than embedded practice?

2. What systems (onboarding, performance, promotion, recognition) are currently aligned with your values – and which ones need to change?

3. Which leadership behaviours are reinforcing the Five Pillars – and which are quietly eroding them?

4. Who are the culture stewards in your organization – and are they empowered to protect meaning?

5. If you were to leave your role tomorrow, what parts of your culture would endure? What would fade? And what does that say about what's embedded?

Chapter 10
Leading meaningful change – from resistance to resilience

'Change is hard because people don't resist change –
they resist loss.'
Ronald Heifetz

Summary

Now we explore one of the most important – and misunderstood – elements of cultural transformation:

Why do people resist change? And how can meaning help them move through it?

Sarah is at a critical midpoint in the journey. The Meaning Metrics dashboard is live. The Lead with Meaning playbook is rolling out. But friction is rising. Some managers are hesitant. A few teams are drifting. And Giovanni – once vocal about prioritizing results over emotion – now reaches out, having encountered unexpected cultural pushback in his own change efforts.

Angela introduces a new lens: 'People don't resist change. They resist meaninglessness.'

This insight comes from her experience leading Project Morpheus – a transformation initiative launched during her time in global technology consulting. Morpheus was designed to deliver agile innovation and cultural renewal. But what ultimately drove its success wasn't the strategy or the structure. It was the way people found meaning inside the change. That's where Angela's approach was crystallized – and why this chapter exists.

We draw from classic and contemporary change literature as a map for why meaning is a precondition for sustainable transformation:

- Kotter (1996) reminds us that the change must start with shared purpose and end with culture. Meaning provides the emotional anchor across all eight steps.

- Beckhard and Harris (1987) show that people resist when the vision isn't clear or personal. Meaning makes the destination *matter*.

- Bridges (2009) teaches that it's not the change itself that trips people – it's the emotional transitions. Meaning helps people make sense of what's ending and what's beginning.

- Avey et al. (2008) offer Psychological Capital (PsyCap) – hope, efficacy, resilience and optimism – as the resources people draw upon to move through uncertainty. Meaning, Angela argues, is what fuels those resources.

- Folger and Skarlicki (1999) show that resistance often arises when people perceive change as violating fairness or values. Meaning restores integrity.

We also bring in Crum, Salovey and Achor (2013) and Dweck's (2006) growth mindset research to show that people are more resilient – and more adaptive – when change is framed as purposeful, not just necessary.

Angela reframes the leadership objective: it's not to eliminate resistance. It's to replace fear with meaning – and help people locate their own story inside the change.

For Sarah, this becomes a strategic turning point.

She stops asking: *How do I get people on board?*

And starts asking: *How do I help people feel part of something worth changing for?*

The change is working – but friction is rising

Sarah leaned back in her chair, scanning the latest pulse dashboard. The indicators were holding steady: Engagement 76%, Meaningful Work Index 72%, Psychological Safety trending upward.

But the story underneath was more complicated.

Two of her highest-performing teams had recently missed major milestones. A director in the operations function had quietly raised concerns about change fatigue. And in a skip-level meeting, a team lead had voiced what others were likely thinking:

'There's a lot of language around meaning. But sometimes it feels like more pressure – not more purpose.'

Sarah frowned. They had come so far. The Five Pillars were visible in rituals. Leaders were applying the Lead with Meaning playbook. The Meaning Metrics dashboard was in use.

This wasn't active resistance anymore. It was emotional drift – the kind of quiet disengagement that Meaning Metrics could detect, but dashboards still missed.

That afternoon, she received a message from Giovanni.

> *Sarah – quick question. How do you know when cultural change is actually sticking? We're seeing a lot of surface-level adoption. But beneath that, it's… murky. Curious how you've handled the drop-off.*

This was new. Giovanni had always been confident. Outcome-driven. Dismissive of cultural nuance. But something had shifted. And now, instead of issuing statements, he was asking questions.

Sarah replied:

> *It's not about resistance. It's about emotional meaning.*
>
> *Let's talk.*

The next day, she met with Angela to unpack what was happening – not just in response to Giovanni's note, but across her own organization.

'We've done so much,' Sarah said. 'Why does it still feel fragile?'

Angela nodded, unsurprised.

'Because strategy doesn't make culture stick. Meaning does. And meaning takes a different kind of leadership.'

She paused, then pulled out a file.

'I want to tell you about a project I led – it's where a lot of the foundations of this approach comes from.'

She placed a one page document on the table, at the top of it was the heading: Project Morpheus.

Angela explained.

It had been a multi-year transformation initiative in a global organization – a change effort designed to accelerate innovation and simplify operations. But early on, they hit a wall. Engagement dropped. Resentment grew. Leaders followed the new structure, but emotionally, people had checked out.

'That initiative,' Angela explained, 'was where I realized the central truth of leading culture change: people don't resist change. They resist meaninglessness.'

What changed everything wasn't just a better strategy. It was the decision to treat culture not as a message – but as a system. They embedded the Five Pillars, trained leaders using an early version of the Lead with Meaning playbook, and tracked culture shifts with precursors to today's Meaning Metrics.

Angela's team began redesigning the change programme to help people find personal connection to the mission, to their teams and to their own contribution. They layered in the very tools that would later become the Five Pillars, the Lead with Meaning playbook and the Meaning Metrics.

'When people understood *why* the change mattered to them and saw progress in their own development,' Angela said, 'they stopped resisting. They started rebuilding.'

That was the breakthrough. And it was what made Angela realize that most change efforts fail not because of poor planning – but because people can't feel themselves inside the change.

Sarah underlined that idea in her notebook: *Change fails when it lacks emotional meaning.*

This wasn't just another project for her team. It was the moment the culture would either embed – or begin to erode.

And if she wanted resilience, she needed to lead the next phase differently.

Not with urgency. But with meaning.

The resistance isn't personal – it's psychological

The next morning, Sarah met with Angela in one of the breakout rooms just off the main leadership suite.

She pulled up a chair, frustration still lingering.

'Some of the leaders are doing everything we've asked. But they're still getting resistance from their teams. It's quiet. But it's there.'

Angela didn't flinch.

'Of course it is,' she said. 'Because resistance isn't a sign of failure. It's a sign of emotional disruption. And if we don't lead people through that, they'll survive the change but disengage from the culture.'

She flipped open her notebook.

'Let's break it down.'

Angela drew a simple triangle on the page, writing a phrase at each point:

- Fear of loss
- Loss of control
- Loss of meaning

'These,' she said, 'are the real reasons people resist change. This is why the Ecosystem matters. If the structure doesn't support the emotional journey, the change will always feel like a threat.'

She cited Beckhard and Harris (1987), who argued that resistance is strongest when people don't understand the need for change, can't see the destination or feel left out of the process. It's not about stubbornness, it's about disconnection.

Then she drew a second triangle – inverted – overlaying it with what she called the meaning-based antidotes:

- Personal purpose
- Progress and agency
- Emotional safety

'When people feel part of something bigger, see themselves getting better and know they won't be punished for feeling unsure – they move.'

Sarah nodded. She'd seen it herself.

Angela brought up Bridges' (2009) model of transition – ending, neutral zone, new beginning – and explained that most change efforts over-focus on the external shift and under-focus on the emotional journey.

'Change is situational,' Angela said, 'but transition is psychological. And meaning is what helps people cross the bridge.'

Sarah remembered one of her own team leads – a capable, high-performing manager – who had said during a check-in: 'It's not that I disagree with where we're going. I just can't see where I fit anymore.'

That was the moment Sarah realized the resistance wasn't about disagreement.

It was about identity.

Angela confirmed it with research. Folger and Skarlicki (1999) found that when change feels misaligned with values – even if it's strategically sound – people resist not out of rebellion, but out of psychological self-protection.

'This is why we focus on meaning,' Angela said. 'Because meaning is what rebuilds trust – when structure isn't enough.'

Sarah took a deep breath.

'So if I want them to stay with me, I have to help them feel something personal. Not just professional.'

Angela smiled.

'Exactly. Culture isn't what converts people. Meaning does.'

Sarah closed her notebook.

This wasn't about 'getting buy-in.' It was about helping people find their own reason to move forward.

Meaningful change doesn't begin with execution. It begins with emotional orientation. And that's what Angela had helped Sarah to lead.

How meaning builds resilience – the science and the story

Later that week, Sarah walked into a regional town hall. It had been a turbulent quarter – system updates, structure shifts, a long-awaited product launch. She opened the session with a simple question:

'What's keeping you going?'

The responses were quiet at first. But then came the truth:

'Knowing I'm still growing.'

'My manager's been checking in – that's helped.'

'We've been stretched – but it still feels like it matters.'

Sarah smiled. It wasn't the absence of stress that made these teams resilient. It was the presence of meaning.

Angela had framed it clearly in their last 1:1. 'Resilience isn't just bouncing back. It's finding energy through meaning when things are hard.'

She introduced a body of research called Psychological Capital – or PsyCap (Luthans, Youssef and Avolio, 2007). It includes four capacities:

1. Hope – belief in a better outcome

2. Efficacy – confidence in your ability to affect change

3. Resilience – ability to recover from setbacks

4. Optimism – positive expectation that effort will be worth it

Angela explained that the Five Pillars were the psychological nutrients that allowed PsyCap to grow, especially under pressure.

PsyCap had become a core element of NexusNova's leadership training – paired with the Lead with Meaning playbook and reinforced in Meaning

Metrics tracking. It gave language to what many leaders instinctively felt: that when people understand the *why*, they stretch further, last longer and recover faster.

Angela backed it with research from Avey et al. (2008), who showed that the value of PsyCap were linked to greater openness to change, higher performance and lower cynicism during transformation.

Sarah also began exploring the role of mindset in how teams responded to pressure. She drew from Dweck's (2006) work on growth mindset – the belief that abilities can be developed through effort and learning. Teams with growth mindset didn't fear failure. They saw it as feedback. And when paired with purpose, they became not just more resilient, but more innovative.

'People don't burn out from change,' Angela had told her. 'They burn out from meaningless change.'

Angela also introduced a more subtle idea – the stress mindset. Drawing on research by Crum, Salovey and Achor (2013), she explained that stress isn't always negative. When people perceive the stress of change as a sign of growth, rather than a threat, they become more focused, resourceful and creative.

'It's not just about reducing pressure,' Angela said. 'It's about reframing pressure as purposeful. And this is where rituals matter: in the middle of change, small moments – like recognizing progress or reconnecting to purpose – help people hold their footing.'

Sarah tested this with her team, sharing the story of Project Morpheus, where teams thrived not because change was easy, but because it was framed as meaningful. Every ritual, every update, every feedback loop connected back to purpose and progress.

'We said to people: "This is hard. But it's worth it. And here's how you're growing."'

The results spoke for themselves.

Now, Sarah was seeing the same possibility take root in her own company.

Sarah leaned back as her team wrapped up the town hall.

'This isn't resilience from toughness,' she thought. 'This is resilience from knowing why we're here.'

And that, she now knew, was her new leadership responsibility.

Not just to explain the change. But to help people feel strong enough to live it.

Leading the dip – what Sarah and Giovanni learn about sustainable change

Two weeks later, Sarah and Giovanni met for a quiet breakfast.

There were no press, no consultants. Just two leaders comparing notes on what it actually takes to lead meaningful change.

'We've done all the right things,' said Giovanni. 'Vision, values, structure. But it's stalling. I'm seeing cynicism – not from the usual sceptics, but from our best people.'

Sarah nodded. She'd been there. And still was, in moments.

'We've seen the same,' she said. 'And we've learned that what stalls change isn't lack of alignment. It's loss of meaning in the middle.'

Giovanni raised an eyebrow. Sarah continued.

'We were measuring adoption. We should have been measuring energy.'

Angela had a name for it: 'the dip'.

'This is where most transformations die,' Angela had said. 'Not because the logic is wrong – but because leaders stop reinforcing the emotional meaning of the work.'

She drew on Kotter's (1996) idea of building short-term wins – not just for optics, but to maintain belief. She paired it with Amabile and Kramer's (2011) *The Progress Principle*, showing that small wins weren't just motivational. They were meaning restorers.

'In the dip,' Angela said, 'your job as a leader is to narrate purpose and spotlight progress. Constantly.'

Sarah began intentionally designing dip rituals – moments where teams were reminded not just of progress, but of purpose. She used the Lead with Meaning playbook anchor of 'Framing the Why' to ground updates, and highlighted Growth and Connection from the Meaning Metrics to track emotional resilience.

These weren't campaign artefacts. They were cultural signals.

Giovanni leaned forward.

'So you're saying… the drop in energy isn't failure. It's the place where leaders have to dig deeper?'

Sarah smiled.

'Exactly. And that digging has to be done through meaning – not just messaging.'

Angela had framed it this way: 'You don't push people through the dip. You lead them through it – by helping them feel part of a meaningful path forward.'

Together, Sarah and Giovanni mapped out what Angela called dip rituals – leadership actions that helped sustain culture when belief wavered:

- Reframing stress as a signal of growth (Crum et al., 2013)

- Using Meaning Metrics to track not just morale, but Alignment, Growth, Connection and Resonance

- Protecting core rituals (like recognition, learning, feedback) even during deadlines

- Making meaning visible through progress stories, not just data

- Training mid-level leaders to lead transitions emotionally, not just structurally (Bridges, 2009)

Giovanni closed his notebook.

'I used to think culture at work was a "nice-to-have"', he said. 'Now I'm realizing it's what makes strategy stick.'

Sarah looked at him. 'Welcome to the long game.'

Angela had mapped it on a visual during Project Morpheus that she shared with Sarah. 'We don't just change behaviour,' she said. 'We move through emotion. And that movement has a rhythm.'

Figure 14 presents the Meaningful Change Curve – the emotional arc teams experience when shifting from purpose rhetoric to meaningful work reality.

Employee Response

	Shock	Cynicism	Fatigue	Experimentation	Commitment
Employee	Confusion, fear	Resistance, sarcasm	Burnout, apathy	Tentative engagement	Hope, motivation
Inner narrative	'Wait! What's happening?'	'Here we go again'	'I'm tired, feels like extra work'	'I'm willing to try'	'It's working, this is how we are now'
Risk	Withdrawal, silence	Erosion of trust	Quiet quitting	Fragile confidence	Regression if unsupported
Leadership Actions	Model vulnerability normalise uncertainty	Translate why the change matters	Coach for resilience and energy	Celebrate small wins, support autonomy	Reinforce purpose and community

Figure 14: The Meaningful Change Curve outlines six predictable phases in a change journey: shock → cynicism → fatigue → experimentation → commitment → integration. Recognizing these stages helps leaders normalize resistance, support meaning-making, sustain momentum and embed new behaviours over time.

The Lead with Meaning playbook, the Meaningful Work Ecosystem, the Meaning Metrics weren't abstract tools anymore. They were how leaders carried people through the dip – in the Meaningful Change Curve – through disorientation, resistance and fatigue - anchored by trust, guided by meaning and fuelled by momentum. It wasn't about bypassing discomfort. It was about walking through it with purpose.

Final Reflection

As Sarah left the breakfast meeting with Giovanni, she felt a quiet conviction settling in. They hadn't cracked the code but they were both asking better questions now.

Not 'How do we roll this out faster?' but 'How do we help people carry this for longer?'

Sarah smiled. The old leadership playbook had taught her to drive urgency. But this chapter of her journey had taught her something more enduring: when people feel meaning, they don't need pushing – they move forward willingly.

Angela had said it simply: 'If your strategy is ambitious, your culture has to be resilient. And meaning is what makes it so.'

Sarah saw it now with new clarity. The reason so many change efforts failed wasn't that people resisted direction – it was that they resisted disconnect. The loss of control. The loss of identity. The loss of emotional clarity.

Meaning restored those things.

Not by pretending change wasn't hard. But by making it matter.

'Change doesn't fail because people can't do it,' she wrote in her notebook. 'It fails because they can't feel *why it's worth it.*' And that, she now knew, was where her real work began.

Now came the next challenge: how to scale that leadership beyond the pilot phase, across countries, teams and systems without losing the meaning they had worked so hard to build.

Change had begun. But sustaining it across geographies, across systems and across generations would be the real test.

In the next chapter, they'd explore how to scale meaningful work enterprise-wide, so it didn't depend on Sarah, or Angela or any one team. It would live in the fabric of the organization.

Takeaways

- Resistance is not personal – it's psychological. People resist change not because they're stubborn, but because they can't see themselves inside the change. Meaning reduces resistance by restoring personal purpose, clarity and safety (Beckhard and Harris, 1987; Folger and Skarlicki, 1999; Bridges, 2009).

- Change isn't just structural – it's emotional. Leading change requires helping people to navigate endings, uncertainty and new beginnings. Meaning provides emotional orientation and continuity (Bridges, 2009; Cameron and Green, 2015).

- Meaning builds resilience. Psychological Capital (PsyCap) – hope, efficacy, resilience and optimism – is fuelled by meaningful work. People become more adaptive when they understand the purpose behind the pressure (Avey et al., 2008; Dweck, 2006; Crum et al., 2013).

- Sustainable change needs cultural rhythm. Leaders must reinforce meaning through consistent rituals, visibility of progress and emotionally intelligent communication. The dip in energy is not failure – it's the moment that meaning must be made visible again (Kotter, 1996; Amabile and Kramer, 2011).

- Meaning is what makes change hold. Strategies will evolve, structures will shift. But when people experience meaning in how the change is led, they build belief, not just compliance. And that's what makes it last.

Reflection Questions

1. Where in your organization are people showing signs of resistance – and what might they be missing in terms of meaning, not information?

2. How are you helping teams see purpose and progress, not just plans and deadlines?

3. What are the small rituals or behaviours your leaders can use to build emotional connection and cultural resilience during change?

4. Who is narrating the 'why' behind your current changes – and are they doing it through stories, not just strategies?

5. If someone asked your employees 'Is this change meaningful to you?' – what would they say?

Chapter 11
Scaling meaningful work across the enterprise

'For individuals, character is destiny. For organizations,
culture is destiny.'
Tony Hsieh, former CEO of Zappos

Summary

Now we confront a question that many organizations never ask soon
enough: *Can our culture scale as fast as our business?*

Sarah's company is expanding – new geographies, new leadership layers
and new hires arriving every week. The Five Pillars of Meaningful Work
have been embraced in pilot teams. The Lead with Meaning playbook
is now core to leadership training. Meaning Metrics are embedded in
dashboards.

But the challenge now isn't traction. It's consistency without rigidity.

Angela reframes the question of scale. This isn't about rolling out a
universal programme. It's about ensuring that meaning scales without
becoming diluted.

We draw from powerful models in organizational design and growth:

- Sutton and Rao's (2014) concept of 'Catholicism vs. Buddhism' – the difference between codifying practices vs spreading principles

- Schneider, Ehrhart and Macey (2013) on how subcultures form and what leaders can do to align climate and culture as scale increases

- Meyer's (2014) culture map on how meaning must be localized in global expansion

- Netflix (Hastings and Meyer, 2020) as a case of radical cultural clarity at scale

- Cameron and Quinn's (2011) cultural diagnostics to support system-wide alignment

- Case studies from KPMG, Zappos and AXA, showing how values like purpose and meaning have scaled to tens of thousands of employees

Angela also shares lessons from Project Morpheus and latter change programmes – how system-wide cultural alignment was sustained across several countries and what it taught her about scaling through stewardship, not slogans.

For Sarah, this chapter is a test of leadership maturity. Can she move from change champion to culture steward? And can her organization now lead with meaning – everywhere?

This chapter shows how.

The strategy is scaling – but is the culture?

Sarah stood at the front of a welcome session for 48 new NexusNova hires.

The room was bright, the energy high. The culture video had just finished playing – soaring music, bold statements, smiling faces, scenes from offices around the world. The Five Pillars appeared at the end, accompanied by the company purpose and a few short testimonials.

Everyone clapped. But as Sarah scanned the room, something shifted inside her. It wasn't wrong. But it wasn't embodied. It echoed the values, but not yet the energy.

Later that afternoon, she note to herself that to scale culture, they couldn't rely on tone or personality. They had to build it into the operating system.

In recent months, NexusNova had experienced accelerated growth:

- Four new markets opened

- Two major acquisitions announced

- 500+ new hires added in 90 days

- An entirely new layer of senior leadership recruited

From a business perspective, it was a win. From a cultural perspective, Sarah could feel the strain.

In some teams, the Five Pillars were visible. Managers still opened stand-ups with 'Why does this work matter?' Rituals were being repeated. Storytelling was happening.

But in others? Some of the drivers of meaningful work in the Five Pillars were being challenged. Autonomy was collapsing under control. Connection was surface-level. Impact was no longer visible in the pressure to deliver.

Angela had warned her about this. During their last debrief, she'd said: 'Culture at scale either spreads through stewardship or dilutes through drift.'

She referenced Schein's (2010) warning that as organizations grow, subcultures form and without intentional alignment, they begin to rewrite the norms.

Angela wasn't advocating uniformity. She was advocating intentionality – and the courage to codify what mattered most before it diluted.

'Your culture isn't what happens in HQ anymore,' she said. 'It's what gets repeated, adapted and protected – everywhere.'

Giovanni echoed the concern in a message later that week.

We've rolled out our own purpose and leadership behaviours. But I'm already seeing three versions forming – sales, ops and regional markets. And I'm not sure which one we're reinforcing.

Sarah replied with a single line: 'Then it's time to shift from diffusion to design.'

That week, Angela brought the executive team together.

She opened with a prompt: 'Let's assume the business will double in size in the next three years. Can your culture double with it?'

The silence was telling.

Some leaders had built rituals into their teams. Others hadn't. Some departments had internalized the Five Pillars. Others still relied on personal interpretation. Global teams had started adapting language. The meaning was there – but it was beginning to fracture.

Angela underlined a single sentence:

'Meaning at scale must be consistent in intent – but flexible in expression.'

This was the leadership shift Sarah had been sensing. They were no longer culture *creators*. They were now culture *stewards*.

And that, she realized, was an even bigger responsibility.

Designing for scale – codifying what's sacred, localizing what's not

Two weeks later, Angela led a working session with NexusNova's senior leadership team.

The prompt on the screen read:

'What is sacred? What can flex?'

'The Five Pillars, the Lead with Meaning playbook, the Meaning Metrics – these aren't just models,' Angela said. 'They're anchors. But they only work if your people know where they flex and where they don't.'

She'd used this exercise many times – first during Project Morpheus and now with clients scaling at pace. It was deceptively simple. But it surfaced what mattered most.

Angela began with a caution. 'Scaling isn't about replication. It's about intention. And if you don't define what's sacred, everything starts adapting. Until you've scaled... nothing.'

She referenced Sutton and Rao's (2014) concept of Buddhism vs. Catholicism in cultural scaling. Catholicism, they argued, was about consistency – codifying practices, enforcing rituals. Buddhism was about principles – teaching intent, then letting practice emerge locally.

'Your job,' Angela said, 'isn't to write a script. It's to define the truths you won't compromise on – and the language others are free to translate.'

The team began mapping the Five Pillars against the enterprise. They identified a core challenge: in some regions, Autonomy was misread as 'do what you want'. In others, Connection was hard to build across hybrid teams and language differences. Impact was deeply felt in client-facing roles – but nearly invisible in back-office functions.

Angela introduced the Design for Meaning at Scale matrix – a tool she'd built during Project Morpheus. It included three levels of meaning integration:

1. Codify what's core (e.g., the Five Pillars, Lead with Meaning playbook).

2. Localize how it's expressed (rituals, language, examples).

3. Measure consistency through Meaning Metrics.

They agreed that Meaning Metrics would now be used not just for tracking sentiment but for managing integrity. If Connection dropped in a new hub or Resonance flatlined in a function, that was a signal the system needed support.

She referenced Erin Meyer's (2014) culture map, reminding the group that what feels meaningful in the UK may not land the same way in India, Tokyo, São Paulo or Berlin.

'You're not just scaling culture,' Angela said. 'You're scaling emotional resonance across contexts.'

Sarah could see the power – and the complexity.

'This isn't a rollout,' Sarah said. 'It's a full-stack cultural operating system – one where strategy, systems, rituals and stories reinforce the same truth.'

Angela nodded, referencing Bartlett and Ghoshal (1998) on managing across borders. Their insight: global alignment doesn't come from uniformity. It comes from shared purpose, empowered local leadership and systems that reinforce values, not control.

The team began codifying:

- The Five Pillars: non-negotiable anchors
- The Lead with Meaning playbook: taught universally, applied contextually
- Rituals: flexible based on geography, but reinforced monthly
- Metrics: tracked globally with space for regional storytelling

Angela offered one final insight: 'When culture scales well, you don't just teach behaviours. You teach beliefs.'

And that, Sarah realized, was the new Lead with Meaning playbook. Not for what people should do. But for what leaders should protect – wherever they were.

Scaling through stories, systems and stewards

Sarah stood in front of the board with a single statement on the slide:

Culture doesn't scale by accident. It scales through design.

It had been four months since the executive workshop on cultural integrity. Since then, NexusNova had opened three new regional hubs, launched two new product lines and onboarded over 1,000 new employees. They had every reason to celebrate.

But Sarah wasn't there to talk about numbers. She was there to talk about the system that would protect their soul. Angela had helped her structure the scale strategy around three reinforcing levers:

1. Stories – the carriers of culture

'People don't remember frameworks,' Angela said. 'They remember stories.'

Together, they'd introduced a global 'meaning moments' campaign – a storytelling initiative across all regions. Teams were invited to share brief narratives about where they had felt one of the Five Pillars activated in their work: a moment of trust, a breakthrough in growth, a moment of impact.

These were published in town halls, rolling vignettes linked to each of the Five Pillars on the intranet, Yammer feeds and in onboarding decks as cultural reference points. These meaning moments were curated to reflect not only values alignment, but also the Five Pillars in action. That's what made them contagious.

Angela referenced Zappos and Netflix as organizations that scaled culture by codifying their stories into onboarding, recruitment and performance. Netflix's culture deck was not just famous because of what it said – but because it consistently reinforced how to behave.

'Stories create memory,' Angela said. 'And memory creates consistency.'

These weren't just warm anecdotes. They were meaning activators – helping new hires, leaders and regions absorb culture not through instruction, but through feeling.

2. Systems – the infrastructure of belief

Sarah's team expanded the Meaning Metrics dashboard across all regions. This allowed them to track cultural consistency alongside business performance.

Angela brought in research from Cameron and Quinn (2011) and the Competing Values Framework, showing how organizations could be both adaptable and coherent if they built systems that connected individual experience to organizational values.

'Scaling isn't about removing uniqueness,' she said. 'It's about making the core experience recognizable – even in new forms.'

Rituals were formalized across markets – opening meetings with 'Why it matters', embedding reflection prompts in stand-ups, redesigning 1:1 templates to include pillar check-ins.

Global HR leads were empowered to localize messaging – but always anchored to the same foundation:

- What's meaningful here?
- How are we living it?
- Where is it breaking down?

This also allowed for meaning localization – different expressions, same principles. The ecosystem held the structure; the rituals brought it to life.

3. Stewards – the protectors of culture

The linchpin was the Culture Steward Network – not a programme, but a social operating system. These stewards weren't just symbolic. They were trained to recognize drift, elevate story and reinforce the Lead with Meaning playbook in daily practice. They met quarterly to:

- Share cultural insight
- Identify early signs of drift
- Surface rituals worth scaling
- Report to executive leadership with grounded, real-time data

Angela shared examples from KPMG's purpose rollout, where thousands of employees wrote personal statements linking their roles to a larger purpose. That campaign didn't just inspire people – it institutionalized belief.

'Stewards aren't champions,' Angela said. 'Champions inspire. Stewards protect.'

Sarah stood at the front of the board and closed with one final statement:

'We've invested in performance systems. Now we're investing in what holds them together.'

And in that moment, she wasn't just the CEO of a scaling business.

She was the steward of a culture that was ready to go global – without losing what made it human.

When scale becomes legacy – building culture that outlasts you

The following quarter, Sarah was invited to speak at an industry leadership forum on the topic of culture and growth.

She opened with a question:

'What if culture isn't something you grow alongside the business – but the thing that makes the business grow?'

The room was quiet.

Then she shared the story of NexusNova – how they had begun with bold purpose statements, shifted into the Five Pillars to make meaning actionable, developed new leadership capabilities through the Lead with Meaning playbook, embedded Meaning Metrics to track what truly mattered, and scaled the Meaningful Work Ecosystem across continents.

The result wasn't just cultural alignment. It was performance resilience. Engagement and collaboration increased and teams shared that they didn't just understand the strategy, they believed in it.

'But what made it sustainable,' she said, 'wasn't just structure. It was stewardship.'

That idea had become her new anchor.

It was no longer about maintaining cultural tone. It was about sustaining cultural muscle – and ensuring the system didn't rely on Sarah's presence to hold.

Angela had framed it this way during their last strategic offsite:

'Culture becomes legacy when it stops depending on the senior leader's energy – and starts living in the design.'

Sarah wrote that on the whiteboard in capital letters:

Legacy isn't charisma. It's architecture

They began building a simple but powerful tool: a Cultural Continuity framework – codifying not just *what* made the culture meaningful, but *how* it would be protected across:

- Successions and leadership transitions
- Market pivots and product evolution
- Mergers and acquisitions integrations
- Future crises

Angela shared insights from Collins and Porras (1994) that the companies which endure aren't those with the flashiest cultures, but those with deeply embedded core values and purpose, protected through every decision, reward system and policy.

She also cited Higgins (2005), whose 'Eight S's' of strategy execution included shared values as the linchpin of alignment during scale and complexity.

Sarah wrote the question that had quietly shaped her past year: *If I stepped away tomorrow – would the culture still hold?* And now, she could finally say 'yes.' That, she realized, was the test of whether the culture had scaled – or whether it had just followed her shadow.

Angela reminded her: 'You're not building a culture that needs you. You're building one that will outlast you.'

That changed how Sarah thought about every system, every ritual, every leader she promoted.

It wasn't just about what would work today. It was about what would endure long after she was gone.

Sarah looked out across the room – at leaders who had once been sceptical, silent, or simply surviving. Now they were shaping culture, not just talking about it. They weren't holding meaning at the top. They were growing it everywhere.

This wasn't about sustaining her legacy. It was about building a system that didn't need her to hold.

And that was the legacy: A culture powered not by performance targets or slogans, but by leaders and teams who knew how to lead with meaning – together.

Final Reflection

As Sarah closed her laptop at the end of the global strategy meeting, she glanced at the whiteboard behind her.

Someone had written a quote during the session:

We don't want a bigger culture. We want a deeper one.

She left it there. It captured everything they were building now. Not faster growth at the cost of meaning – but growth *because* of meaning. Not perfect consistency – but resilient clarity.

Angela had said it best: 'You're not scaling a brand. You're scaling belief. And belief spreads not through control, but through trust.'

Sarah looked around the quiet room – now filled with stories, systems and stewards. The culture wasn't being driven anymore. It was being held. And that, she realized, was what leadership had become.

Not broadcasting the vision. But protecting what mattered – so that others could carry it forward.

Takeaways

- Scaling culture is a leadership responsibility. Culture doesn't expand by accident – it grows through stewardship. Leaders need to intentionally codify what's sacred, localize what's flexible and reinforce values through systems and behaviour (Schein, 2010; Sutton and Rao, 2014; Cameron and Quinn, 2011).

- Meaning can scale but it needs to be designed to travel. Organizations scale meaning by embedding the Five Pillars of Meaningful Work, reinforcing the Lead with Meaning playbook and tracking culture through Meaning Metrics across all levels and geographies.

- Systems sustain what slogans cannot. The organizations that maintain culture at scale align stories, rituals, recognition and feedback to protect meaning, as shown in case studies like Netflix, Zappos and KPMG's purpose campaign (Hastings and Meyer, 2020; Hsieh, 2010).

- Stewards are the carriers of culture. Scaling culture isn't just about champions or comms. It's about identifying and empowering people across the business who live the values, protect the rituals and elevate local innovation (Collins and Porras, 1994; Bartlett and Ghoshal, 1998).

- Legacy isn't what you leave behind. It's what keeps going without you. When meaning is embedded into the way an organization thinks, acts and grows, it doesn't just scale. It endures.

Reflection Questions

1. Where in your organization is culture already scaling – and where is it starting to drift?

2. What core behaviours, rituals and beliefs must remain sacred – no matter how much you grow?

3. How are you helping new leaders, teams and regions carry the Five Pillars in a way that is true to both the business and their own context?

4. What systems (hiring, onboarding, performance) are currently reinforcing your culture – and which ones are accidentally diluting it?

5. If your leadership team were to change tomorrow, what parts of your culture would endure – and what would fade away? What does that tell you about what you've scaled?

Chapter 12
Meaningful work as a worthy legacy

'Leadership is about making others better as a
result of your presence and making sure that impact
lasts in your absence.'
Sheryl Sandberg

Summary

Finally, we explore the question many leaders avoid – until it becomes
too urgent to ignore:

'What will remain after I'm gone?'

Sarah's transformation is complete. NexusNova has embedded the Five
Pillars of Meaningful Work, scaled the Lead with Meaning playbook,
integrated Meaning Metrics and protected the Meaningful Work
Ecosystem across the enterprise. But now comes the real test:

Can this culture last without her?

Angela helps Sarah shift her thinking one last time – from leading the movement to leaving the movement ready for the future. Scaling meaning wasn't just a growth strategy; it was becoming Sarah's legacy.

We explore legacy on two levels:

1. Organizational: how to build systems, symbols and stories that outlast any one person

2. Personal: how leaders find peace, pride and purpose by investing in a future they may never fully see

This is drawn from:

- Erikson (1959) on generativity – the deep human drive to leave something meaningful behind

- Collins and Porras (1997) on enduring values and core purpose

- Covey (2004) on 'voice and significance' as leadership's highest calling

- Reimer et al. (2020) and Kouzes and Posner (2019) on institutionalizing leadership impact

- Hesselbein and Goldsmith (2006) on serving to live and living to serve

- Obschonka et al. (2017) on values transmission

- Spitzmuller and Stacey (2021) on purpose in late-career transition

Sarah begins thinking about succession – not in terms of replacement, but continuity of meaning. She starts preparing her senior team, empowering mid-level leaders and seeding culture into systems they can protect and evolve.

Angela calls it the Legacy Design Loop – a final framework for ensuring that meaning doesn't fade when the founder or CEO steps away.

Because when legacy is done well, people don't remember just what you built.

They remember how you made work matter. And that, in the end, is a legacy worth leaving.

The work is holding – but what comes next?

Sarah stood in the back of a town hall in NexusNova's new Asia-Pacific hub. She wasn't presenting. She wasn't even scheduled to speak. She was observing. And yet, the moment that followed gave her the clearest answer to a question she hadn't yet asked: 'Could the culture truly scale?' And for the first time, she realized something profound: they didn't need her to translate meaning anymore. They were doing it themselves.

The local managing director stood confidently on stage, walking through the latest results. At the end, he paused.

'I want to close by acknowledging something else. Last month, one of our client teams redesigned their onboarding experience – and used the Five Pillars framework to build trust, purpose and growth into every step. We're seeing the impact already. That's not just a good team. That's a meaningful culture.'

Applause. Smiles. Resonance.

Sarah didn't need to speak. The moment spoke for itself.

'They're carrying it now,' she thought. 'They don't need me to translate meaning anymore.'

And yet, that very realization brought a new question to the surface – quiet, powerful, undeniable: *What happens when I'm gone?*

In a recent check-in, Angela had anticipated the shift. 'You've built the movement. Now you need to think about its continuity. Not just strategy continuity – meaning continuity.'

She handed Sarah a copy of Erikson's *Identity and the Life Cycle*, the pages already annotated:

> *'Generativity is the concern for establishing and guiding the next generation... It encompasses the need to be needed, to care and to leave something behind.'*

Sarah paused on that word – *establishing*. This wasn't just about succession planning. It was about meaning continuity. She was shifting from being the voice of the movement, to preparing others to carry it forward

'Legacy isn't what you leave behind,' Angela said. 'It's what you help others build before you go.'

Over the next few weeks, Sarah started noticing new signs of sustainability:

- Team leads correcting misaligned behaviour with quiet consistency

- Culture stewards using Meaning Metrics to surface local insights

- A manager suggesting a new recognition ritual that tied directly to the Lead with Meaning playbook

- Regional offices adapting language, not discarding principles

The system was holding. The energy was evolving.

'This is what I always hoped would happen,' she thought. 'So why do I feel… unsteady?'

Angela helped her name it: 'Because you're shifting from driving change to distributing stewardship. And that requires a different kind of courage.'

Sarah wrote one line in her notebook:

> *'This isn't the end of the work. It's the beginning of the part that isn't mine.'*

Designing for continuity – the Legacy Design Loop

Angela stood in the leadership suite at NexusNova's headquarters. It was quiet – one of those rare Friday afternoons where the pace had slowed just enough to reflect.

She drew a circle on the whiteboard. Then divided it into four quadrants.

At the centre, she wrote a single word:

'Legacy'

Then around it, she added the four phases of what she called the Legacy Design Loop:

1. Envision the Legacy

2. Engage the Carriers

3. Embed the Essence

4. Evolve and Let Go

'This,' she said to Sarah, 'is how leaders embed meaning so deeply that the culture doesn't just survive them – it becomes stronger because of them.'

Figure 15 shows the Legacy Design Loop – the final step in building a culture that sustains itself through leadership transitions and generational stewardship.

'You've embedded the Five Pillars. You've developed new leadership capabilities with the Lead with Meaning playbook. You've operationalized Meaning Metrics. Now it's time to make sure they endure without relying on your presence,' Angela said.

Sarah stared at the model. It felt clear. And slightly terrifying. She knew what it meant: letting go of ownership and trusting in design.

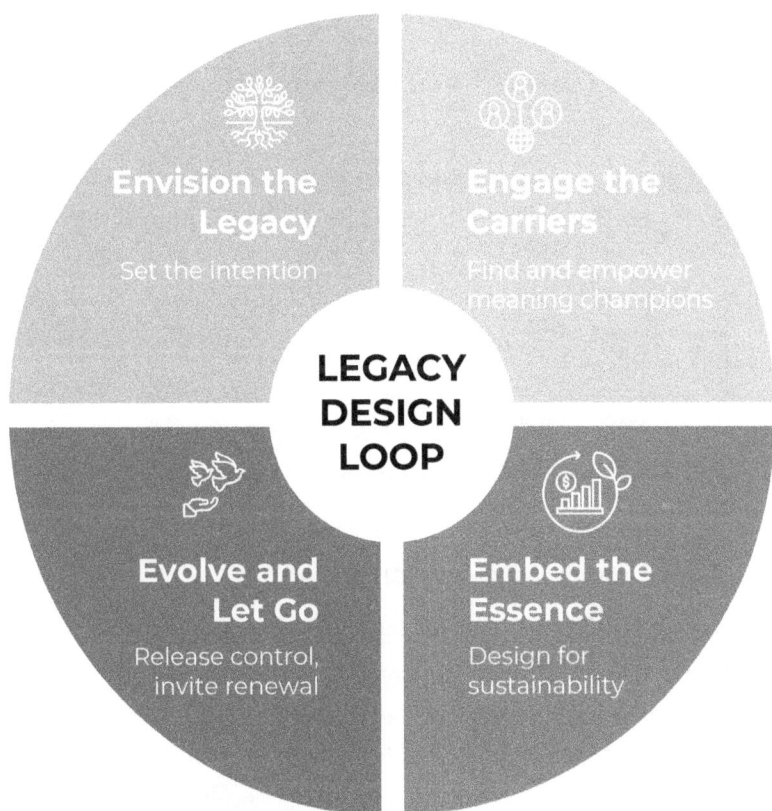

Figure 15: The Legacy Design Loop outlines four phases for embedding a leadership legacy rooted in meaning: Envision the Legacy, Engage the Carriers, Embed the Essence and Evolve and Let Go. Legacy isn't what leaders leave, it's what they help others build before they go.

1. Envision the Legacy – set the intention

Angela began with a question: 'What do you want to leave behind, not as a memory, but as a system?'

They talked about meaning as more than purpose. About legacy as more than succession. Sarah reflected on her own journey – how the work had grown from a personal conviction into a shared, cultural movement.

'Legacy isn't what happens when you leave,' Angela said. 'It starts the moment you begin designing for what will outlast you.'

After some debate and reflection, Sarah crystalized her intent: a culture that would remain coherent, human, and meaningful, no matter who came next.

2. Engage the Carriers – find and empower meaning champions

Next, Angela focused on succession – not just of the CEO, but of culture custodians across the business. 'Legacy isn't about naming a successor. It's about building stewards at every level.'

They mapped key roles – not by job grade, but by impact. These were the 'meaning-makers' – people who kept the ecosystem alive without needing permission.

- Who tells the stories?
- Who models the pillars when no one's watching?
- Who corrects drift without fanfare?

Angela cited Kouzes and Posner (2019):

> 'Your greatest legacy is not your impact. It's the people you equip to have impact long after you're gone.'

Sarah began investing more time with mid-level leaders and culture stewards – those closest to the daily rhythms of meaning.

3. Embed the Essence – design for sustainability

'The first step,' Angela said, 'is to clarify what's sacred – the values, practices and principles that define the meaning you've built.'

Sarah had already codified the Five Pillars, the Lead with Meaning playbook and the cultural design practices. But now, she began refining the 'why' behind them – not just what made them useful, but what made them true.

These weren't just programmes. They were a world view. Her task now was to articulate the cultural DNA – the beliefs that would shape decision-making long after she stepped down.

Angela referenced Collins and Porras's (1997) HBR article 'Building Your Company's Vision,' which argued that enduring companies don't just have clear values – they protect the core ideology through time and turbulence.

Sarah called this her 'cultural inheritance kit' – the truths she wanted every future leader to receive.

4. Evolve and Let Go – release control, invite renewal

This was the hardest phase.

Sarah had been the heartbeat of the movement. Her name was synonymous with the purpose work. Now, Angela challenged her to step back – not out.

'The most meaningful legacies aren't held in authority. They're held in distributed trust.'

They redesigned governance by:

- Giving more autonomy to culture stewards
- Localizing leadership rituals
- Decentralizing story collection and recognition
- Creating a shared ownership board for Meaning Metrics reporting

Angela cited Obschonka et al. (2017), who found that the most enduring cultural legacies are those carried forward through values transmission – not centralized messaging.

Then she went further.

'Legacy doesn't begin when you exit. It begins when you release control but preserve intent.'

Angela drew on Covey's (2004) 8th Habit – the idea that great leaders help others find their voice – and Spitzmuller and Stacey's (2021) research on late-career transition.

Sarah didn't want applause. She wanted continuity.

And the only way to ensure it, was to begin letting go.

With grace.

With pride.

With meaning.

What will outlast you? – legacy through systems, symbols and people

Sarah opened the offsite by saying only this:

'What we build must outlast us. Let's begin there.'

She wasn't there to lead. She was there to observe – and to hand over.

At the centre of the room was a table with three objects:

1. A framed version of the Five Pillars

2. The first Meaning Metrics dashboard ever published

3. A handwritten story from a frontline manager who had joined four years ago and described how 'meaning saved my career here'

Angela opened the session with a question: 'What will outlast us?'

This wasn't theoretical anymore.

Sarah had begun preparing her senior team – not for her departure, but for the reality that succession is not an event. It's a system.

Angela introduced a checklist she'd used with clients preparing for long-term leadership transitions. It included:

- Systems that reinforce values when pressure rises

- Stories that are still being told five years later

- Symbols that carry emotional memory

- Leaders who carry forward not just strategy, but meaning

She referenced Hesselbein and Goldsmith's (2006) *The Leader of the Future*, citing the principle:

> *'To serve is to live. And to serve well is to leave something better than you found it.'*

Sarah underlined one word: 'serve'. They began codifying the final elements of the Meaning Legacy Plan:

Systems

- Codifying how Meaning Metrics were reviewed at board level

- Ensuring the Lead with Meaning playbook integration in every leadership track

- Building a culture health index into performance reviews

- Embedding succession rituals for culture stewards

Symbols

- Launching an annual Meaning in Action recognition award

- Creating a digital 'Story Archive' of cultural turning points

- Designing a ritual where every new hire shares a personal 'why' in their first 90 days

People

- Naming successors not just for roles, but for rituals

- Documenting the founding story of the culture in a form that could be retold

- Empowering community leads to evolve practices over time, without losing intent

Angela reminded the team of Dik and Duffy's (2009) research on calling:

> *'Leaders who see their work as a calling are more likely to build systems that carry meaning forward – because they aren't just trying to lead. They're trying to leave something worthwhile.'*

A legacy wasn't charisma. It was what happened when systems, stories and stewards worked together to protect meaning without needing to name who started it.

Sarah closed her notebook. 'My legacy,' she said, 'isn't what I started. It's what others feel empowered to continue.'

And that, she now knew, was leadership at its highest level.

Final Reflection

Several months later, Sarah walked through the NexusNova atrium as a visitor.

She had officially stepped down as CEO. Her successor – someone she'd helped develop over several years – was now leading the business into its next phase.

No fanfare. No portraits on the wall. Just culture in motion.

She passed a meeting room where a team was reflecting on Meaning Metrics results. In another space, a senior leader was coaching her team through a challenge using the Lead with Meaning playbook. Down the hall, someone was telling a story about how a frontline employee had changed a client's life by showing unexpected care.

None of it was about her. And that, she realized, was the point. When meaning becomes deeply embedded, it doesn't need the founder's voice. It has its own.

And yet… all of it contained her essence.

'This is it,' she thought. 'This is what it means to lead something that lasts.'

Angela's voice echoed back to her, gently but firmly: 'Legacy is what happens when your values keep working – even when you stop.'

Sarah paused by a screen that rotated through new employee stories. One quote caught her eye:

> 'This place helps you grow into who you really are – and lets your work mean something, too.'

No credit line. No headline. But that was the best kind of legacy. The kind that didn't need her name.

Meaning had become self-sustaining. And the next generation of leaders – with Zainab at the helm – was ready to lead it forward. Not as imitators. But as stewards.

If you choose to lead with meaning, you choose a legacy that lasts, in people, in places, in possibilities. Culture is not what you say; it's what you leave behind. And if you get it right, they'll remember how it felt to work with you.

Bringing it all together: the Meaningful Work Hexagon

Together, these elements form a complete operating system designed to embed meaning systemically and sustain it over time.

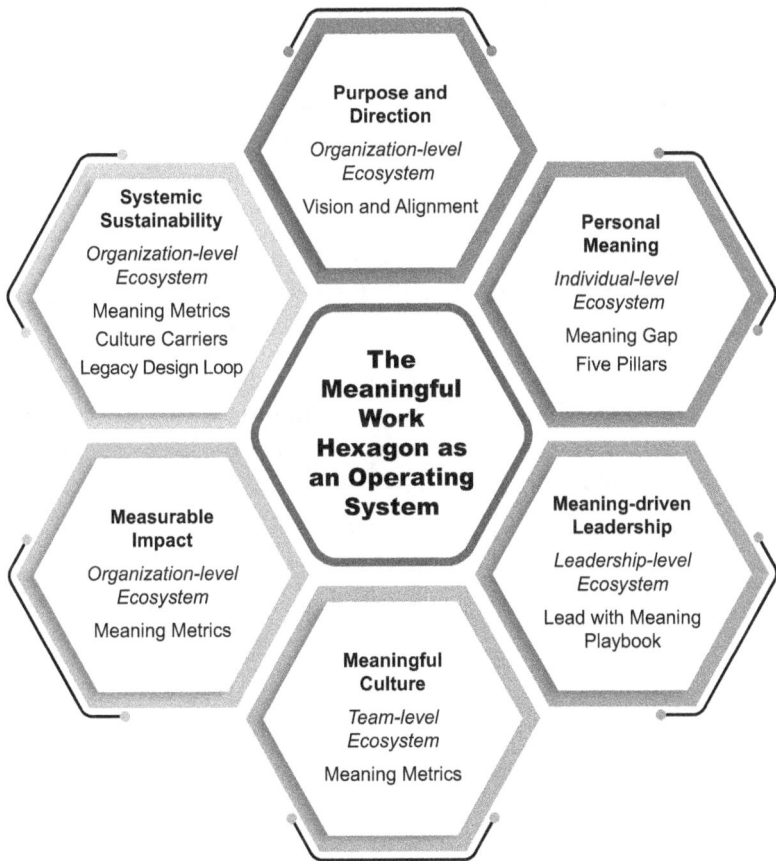

Figure 16: The Meaningful Work Hexagon operating system shows how six strategic capabilities come to life through repeatable frameworks, including the Five Pillars, Meaning Metrics, the Lead with Meaning playbook and the Meaningful Work Ecosystem. Together, they enable leaders to embed meaning systemically, scale it sustainably and translate intent into daily cultural impact.

This final figure brings the entire Meaning Over Purpose system into view. It reminds us that legacy isn't built through intention alone; it's sustained through infrastructure. When leaders embed meaning into daily practices, leadership behaviours, metrics and cultural rhythms, they create the conditions for meaning to last. That's not an end point. It's a design decision.

Takeaways

- Legacy is not an end point. It's a design decision. It begins long before a leader departs – in the way systems, rituals and stewards are prepared to carry meaning forward (Collins and Porras, 1997; Reimer et al., 2020).

- Leaders crave significance – not just success. Erikson's (1959) concept of generativity shows that, in later career stages, people seek to leave behind something meaningful. Legacy work is human development – not just succession planning.

- Meaning is a legacy worth leaving. Great leaders are remembered not for what they controlled, but for what they empowered others to feel and build (Kouzes and Posner, 2019; Covey, 2004).

- A cultural legacy lives in three places: systems, symbols and stewards. When values are protected through structure, rituals and stories, they survive change and adapt over time (Hesselbein and Goldsmith, 2006; Obschonka et al., 2017).

- Your voice can become a movement. When leaders lead with meaning – and design for continuity – their influence becomes less about their presence and more about the purpose they made possible.

Reflection Questions

1. What values or beliefs do you hope will still be alive in your organization ten years from now – and what have you done to embed them?

2. Who are the cultural stewards you are investing in – and how are you preparing them to lead when you're no longer in the room?

3. What systems, stories and rituals are most critical to your cultural legacy – and how are you protecting them from erosion or drift?

4. If someone were to write a sentence about your leadership legacy today, what would it say? What do you hope it will say ten years from now?

5. What are you holding onto that you may need to let go of for your culture to grow beyond you?

Conclusion

The meaningful work revolution

'True leadership is planting trees under whose shade
you do not expect to sit.'
Nelson Henderson

Sarah's closing address

Sarah stood once more before NexusNova's entire leadership community, taking a slow, reflective breath. The auditorium was filled with colleagues who over the years had become true believers and champions of the culture they created together. There was a palpable sense of accomplishment – and anticipation for the future.

'Our journey isn't ending – it's just beginning a new chapter,' Sarah began thoughtfully.

She scanned the sea of familiar faces – faces that had been with her through countless conversations, breakthroughs and even setbacks on the road to meaningful work.

'I no longer need to drive it,' she continued, her voice full of pride. 'Our culture is thriving independently now. The revolution we started – shaping a workplace built around meaningful work – is embedded in our very identity.'

She paused to let the significance sink in. In the front row, Leonie smiled up at her and Sarah noticed many colleagues nodding in agreement. Sarah's voice was steady as she went on. 'Our work now isn't about preserving what we built – it's about continuous evolution. From here forward, our success will be measured not just by profits or growth, but by our ongoing ability to deepen meaning in every interaction, every role, every decision.'

She gestured to the five interlocking rings on a banner behind her – symbolizing NexusNova's Five Pillars.

'Let meaning be your compass,' she said, 'authenticity your strength and legacy your intention. By integrating Autonomy, Mastery, Purpose, Connection and Impact into how we lead, we've proven that meaningful work isn't an idealistic slogan – it's an imperative that unlocks sustainable innovation, resilience and lasting success.' *(See Appendix 3: Personal Meaningful Work Inventory if you're ready to explore what meaningful work means for your own role and career.)*

Heads around the room nodded in agreement. They had lived this truth. It was not theory, but their everyday practice now.

Our Meaning Metrics have shown,' Sarah continued, 'that cultivating meaning doesn't just boost personal fulfilment – it amplifies performance. We haven't implemented just another initiative; we ignited a true revolution in how businesses succeed.'

She looked around, eyes meeting those of individual leaders she had mentored, one by one. In each she saw the spark of ownership. They would carry this forward.

'Meaningful work isn't just what we do – it's who we've become,' she said, her voice momentarily thick with emotion. 'Together, we've created something rare and enduring. And our revolution isn't contained within these walls – it's a model that can inspire organizations globally.'

At that, the room erupted in applause – not the polite clapping of a typical corporate meeting, but a genuine, sustained ovation. It was equal parts gratitude for Sarah's vision and pride in what they had all built. Sarah felt a lump in her throat. This was it – the culmination of dedicated effort. The meaningful work revolution had taken root deeply and now it had a life of its own.

As the applause subsided, Sarah stepped aside from the podium. Standing nearby was Zainab, whom Sarah waved forward. With a warm smile, Sarah placed her company badge – the CEO's badge – into Zainab's hand, a symbolic passing of the torch. The room burst into fresh cheers as the two women shared a brief, heartfelt hug.

Amid genuine applause, Zainab stepped onto the stage – not as a successor to be compared, but as the new CEO fully ready to evolve what had begun. Zainab stepped to the microphone; the room hushed once more. She paused, then smiled.

'This isn't just a leadership change,' she said. 'It's a promise: that what we built here will keep growing – and that every voice will help shape what it becomes.'

The applause returned, this time quieter, steadier – a standing ovation not just for one leader's farewell, but for the rise of the next generation.

Angela, standing at the side of the room, exchanged a glance with Sarah. A small nod passed between them. Unspoken, but understood.

'If your work lives on through others,' Angela had once said, 'then your leadership has done its job.'

Sarah's final reflection

As Sarah left the stage she felt a wave of fulfilment wash over her.

She thought of Angela's guidance, of all the employees whose lives were touched, of the customers benefitting from a deeply engaged and committed workforce – and she thought of the many CEOs out there in the world ready to launch their own meaningful work journeys.

She took a seat, listening as Zainab began to speak of bold evolution and the path ahead. A profound chapter in NexusNova's story was complete, but for the wider world, a new chapter in leadership was unfolding. Sarah knew she would continue to be an ambassador for this cause in her next endeavours. The fire in her heart for meaningful work would never die; she would simply tend it in new ways and places.

Leaning back, Sarah allowed herself a moment of reflection.

'We did it, she thought. We proved that business can be a force for meaning.

Now it's time to spread that message beyond one company.'

Turning her gaze to the back of the room, Sarah imagined for a moment that beyond those doors lay all the leaders reading this book.

To you – yes, you – she silently dedicated this accomplishment.

If we could do it here, you can do it in your organization too.

The baton was now extending far beyond NexusNova. She closed her eyes and smiled, listening to Zainab's strong, confident voice.

'This is what sustainable leadership looks like,' she thought. 'When the mission continues with even more energy under those who follow.'

Her final act as CEO was complete, but her impact would ripple outward for years in the form of a thriving culture – and hopefully, thanks to the book in your hands, in the form of many thriving cultures around the world.

The meaningful work revolution is already underway

The question is no longer *if* it will happen – but *whether you will lead it.*

Whether you're a CEO, a team lead, a coach or a culture architect – your next decision could change someone's experience of work forever.

So, start where you are.

You don't have to lead the whole movement today.

Just begin.

And lead with meaning.

Epilogue
A new era of meaningful leadership

'The best way to predict the future is to create it.'
Peter Drucker

A new CEO, a new chapter

The auditorium buzzed with anticipation. This wasn't just a leadership transition – it was a milestone. Employees from every level, long-time clients and global stakeholders had gathered to witness the passing of the torch from Sarah to Zainab. The energy was electric. At the back of the stage, a bold banner declared:

A New Era for Lead with Meaning

Amid the applause, Zainab stepped forward. Calm, confident, authentic – everything the organization had come to admire about her as COO. Sarah had chosen Zainab not just for her competence, but for her character – and for their shared vision of the future.

Zainab paused before speaking, her gaze steady across the room.

'This isn't just a leadership change,' she said. 'It's a promise: that what we built here will keep growing – and that every voice will help shape what it becomes.'

The applause returned, this time quieter, steadier – a standing ovation not just for one leader's farewell, but for the rise of the next generation.

'It isn't only about continuity,' she continued warmly, 'it's about bold evolution. It's about growing a living legacy,' she said. 'And deepening it for everyone – in every region, every role, every story we tell.'

The tone was familiar – approachable, steady – but now carried the full weight of leadership.

'What Sarah has built here is extraordinary. She showed the world that meaningful work drives business results – engagement, innovation, resilience. Today, we honour that legacy... ' Zainab glanced to Sarah, prompting a fresh round of applause, '... but we also take it forward.'

Zainab honoured the foundation Sarah had built – the Five Pillars, the Lead with Meaning playbook, the Meaning Metrics, the embedded Ecosystem. But she also made something else clear: this was not the ceiling. It was the floor.

'Our mission is no longer just to sustain success,' she said. 'It's to redefine it. To build an inclusive culture where diverse voices don't just contribute – they shape strategy and define our future.'

In that moment, heads lifted. Especially among underrepresented groups, the message impacted deeply: this was their culture too – and now, their future to shape.

Zainab didn't just inspire. She acted. She made a powerful announcement that reinforced her commitment to inclusion:

'From next quarter, every employee, not just managers, will have access to our new self-guided growth programme, Own Your Meaning, designed to help you connect with what matters most, not just for now but for the long haul. It supports your wellbeing, identity and long-term goals. Whether you're early in your career, managing care responsibilities or thinking about what's next, this is about designing work that works for you and grows with you.'

The audience leaned in, energized by the shift. This wasn't just a nod to inclusion, it was an invitation for greater personal agency.

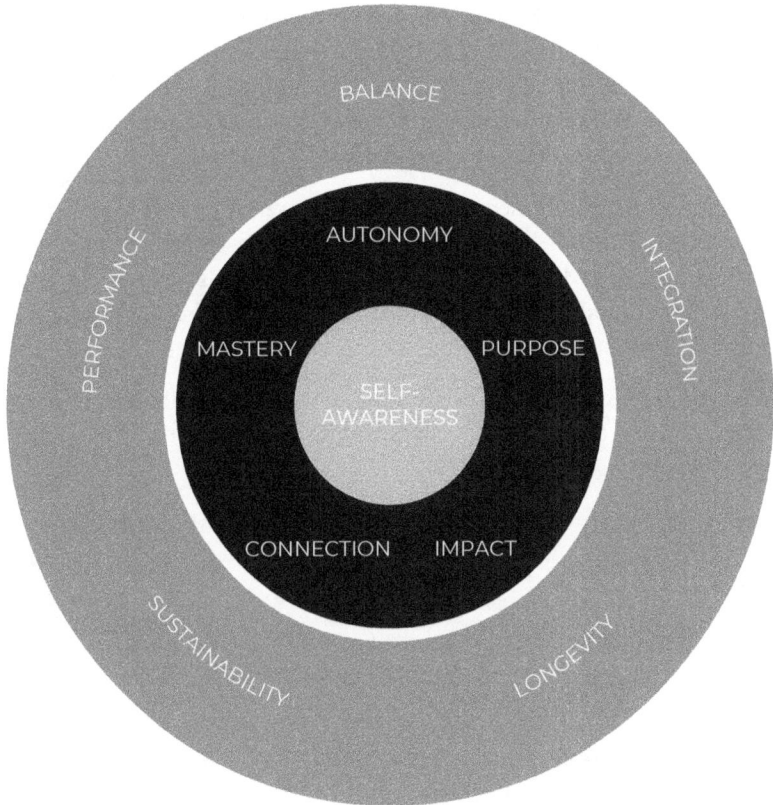

Figure 17: Own Your Meaning helps individuals connect with what matters most – not just for now but for the long haul. Through the lenses of values, growth, contribution and belonging, it supports employees in designing meaningful work that aligns with identity, energy and life stage. Because meaning isn't just about today, it's about building a sustainable, integrated and enduring career.

Zainab believed that the work of meaning didn't belong to leaders alone. It belonged to everyone. Own Your Meaning was built at the intersection of identity, energy, contribution and belonging. When people were invited to define their own meaning, not just absorb someone else's, it didn't just sustain culture. It expanded it.

As the audience hummed with excited conversations about the new investment in people's growth, Zainab went on to announce a new wave of Meaning Metrics tools – real-time dashboards powered by AI to measure inclusion, psychological safety and emotional energy alongside traditional KPIs.

'This tool is designed to track meaning, psychological safety, equity and purpose in real time,' said Zainab. 'We will track whether colleagues feel seen, safe and significant.'

Under Zainab, meaning and inclusion would become the organization's performance system. A ripple of applause turned into a standing ovation.

Sarah watched from the back of the room. And she smiled, not with pride, but with peace. 'This has travelled far beyond me now,' she thought, 'and that's exactly as it should be.'

Purpose may start the journey, but meaning is what carries it forward.

Sarah thought about her own journey. How this phase of leadership felt different from those earlier years of pushing, striving, proving. It wasn't about being the fastest or the boldest anymore. It was about wisdom. Impact. Presence.

She remembered something she'd read recently in Lucy Ryan's research on midlife leadership: 'We must challenge the cultural narrative that midlife marks a decline. For many leaders, it's a launchpad.' (Ryan, 2023).

That insight had stayed with her. Ryan's work explored the often invisible experiences of senior women who had achieved power but not always resonance. Sarah knew that feeling well. There had been moments when she wondered whether her energy was fading or whether the organization had outgrown her. But now, looking at what they'd built, the systems, the succession, the centre, she knew: this was the most meaningful chapter yet.

The shared journey of Sarah and Zainab

Their story had started long before titles – in a mentoring programme where they discovered a shared frustration: that workplaces talked about values but rarely made them felt. Sarah was the mentor, Zainab the mentee – but it didn't take long for the learning to flow both ways.

Over informal coffees and catchups, they discovered a shared belief: that business could be more human-centred. Sarah was grappling with disengagement and quiet attrition in her company. Zainab was navigating a growing sense of mid-career restlessness at another firm.

The turning point came when Zainab joined a research programme led by Angela – a study exploring meaningful work among senior and mid-career women leaders. In a reflective workshop, prompted by Angela's questions, Zainab finally named the tension she'd been feeling: 'My company says all the right things about values – but I don't feel them. And it's breaking my spirit.'

Angela's language – the Meaning Gap, the Five Pillars – gave voice to what Zainab had always sensed. For the first time, she could see what was missing in her own leadership. And what she was called to build.

She brought the concept to a women's leadership forum. Sarah, in the audience, was captivated. Over a follow-up coffee, one conversation became many – deep dialogues about strategy, inclusion and impact. Zainab shared frameworks from Angela's work. Sarah experimented. A pilot giving one team greater autonomy led to a surprising morale boost. Sarah recalled that it was around this time she had engaged Angela for guidance on how to implement meaningful work at NexusNova, and discovered a trusted partner in her, as someone who could support both strategic execution and personal reflection.

As time passed, the mentor–mentee relationship between Sarah and Zainab evolved into a true partnership. Zainab brought an inclusion lens that deeply challenged and enriched Sarah's thinking. She argued that meaning must extend universally – to frontline workers, remote teams and factory staff, not just executives, managers and knowledge workers.

Sarah listened. She shifted. Meaning strategies expanded from the boardroom to the back office. Leadership programmes were redesigned with psychological safety and co-created purpose at the core. It was

Zainab's voice – respectful, consistent – that had helped Sarah build a more holistic, inclusive culture.

When the COO role opened at NexusNova, Sarah didn't hesitate. She didn't just see Zainab as qualified – she saw her as the perfect person who could take the vision further.

Once inside the organization, Zainab became both operational powerhouse and cultural amplifier. She and Sarah worked in harmony – one driving enterprise growth through meaning, the other embedding deep inclusivity into the way NexusNova worked. Angela remained a regular presence, facilitating sessions and evolving the IP with them in real time.

By the time Sarah began planning her exit, the path was clear. Zainab hadn't just earned the role – she had shaped the future it now represented.

As Zainab prepared for her first day as CEO, she turned to Sarah and said quietly: 'I don't just want to sustain what you built. I want to expand it – so every employee, everywhere, feels seen and valued.'

And Sarah, without hesitation, replied: 'You already have.'

Zainab's awakening to meaningful work

Zainab's journey into meaningful work began not with a strategy session or a bold promotion – but with quiet, persistent discontent.

On paper, her career was flawless. She had worked for some great brands, she led high-performing teams, delivered strong results and was widely respected. But inside, something was missing.

'Is this all there is?' she would ask herself on the drive home.

She longed for more than outcomes. She wanted connection. Significance. Integrity.

Early in her career, she'd had mentors who modelled people-first leadership. They taught her that work could be purposeful and that profit didn't need to come at the expense of humanity. But over time, those ideals had faded under the weight of delivery pressure and corporate pragmatism. The spark dimmed.

Her defining wake-up moment came during Angela's research project. In a small focus group of mid-career women, Zainab said: 'I feel like a small cog that doesn't matter. Our mission sounds great. But I don't experience it. We have stated values but I don't feel them in my day-to-day work. And it's breaking my spirit.'

The room was still. Angela gently introduced the term 'meaning gap'. It hit like a lightning bolt.

Zainab suddenly had a name for the ache she'd carried. And, more importantly, she realized she wasn't alone. Her experience wasn't a personal failure. It was systemic.

Angela's frameworks – the Five Pillars, the Purpose-to-Meaning Gap and Meaning Metrics – gave Zainab tools to work with. She went back to her team and began asking different questions:

- Where are we granting autonomy?

- Where do people feel invisible?

- When was the last time we explained why this work matters?

The changes were subtle but immediate. Engagement rose. Tensions eased. A younger team member once said, 'This is the first time I feel like my voice actually matters.' It was proof that small shifts in meaning had exponential returns in inclusion, innovation and morale.

Zainab also began noticing generational patterns. Younger employees weren't just asking for work–life balance – they were asking for work–life *resonance*. Many prioritized impact over title. They wanted growth over hierarchy. They wanted to know their work mattered – and that their workplace *saw* them.

Zainab came to understand a powerful truth: meaning and inclusion are inseparable. If people didn't feel included, their work couldn't be meaningful. And if work lacked meaning, inclusion felt performative.

Leadership, she realized, wasn't about directing from the top. It was about designing from the inside out – creating cultures where everyone could define and discover their own meaning.

When Sarah brought her into NexusNova, Zainab finally found the space to bring these beliefs to life. She had a solid foundation to build on – Sarah had already implemented many meaningful work practices. But under Zainab's influence, inclusion became not an add-on, but a principle of design. Together, they ensured the culture reached every team, every region, every level.

Today, as CEO, Zainab leads with conviction forged through experience – her own, her team's and the voices that once felt unheard. She sees meaningful work not as a leadership trend, but as a human imperative – one that, when done well, unleashes performance, loyalty and possibility in every corner of an organization.

From inclusion to innovation

One of Zainab's first actions as CEO was to articulate her leadership philosophy in a company-wide memo titled:

'Inclusion Through Meaningful Work: A Shared Responsibility.'

In it, she wrote:

'Meaningful work and inclusion are two sides of the same coin. If people do not feel included, their work cannot be truly meaningful. And the most inclusive environments are those where work has deep meaning.'

It became more than a philosophy. It became a strategy – embedded into hiring, onboarding, team rituals, performance systems and product design.

For Zainab, inclusion wasn't a side initiative or an HR compliance checklist. It was embedded in the company's core quest for meaning.

Inclusion meant more than diversity statistics – it meant every employee feeling psychologically safe, valued and inspired to contribute their best. And Angela's data had shown the same: when the Five Pillars are present, inclusion follows.

Autonomy empowers.

Mastery fuels equity in development.

Purpose invites voice.

Connection builds belonging.

Impact validates contribution.

The link was clear. Meaning fosters inclusion – and inclusion deepens meaning. Zainab's realization was simple but profound: *Meaningful work isn't just good for underrepresented groups. It elevates everyone.*

As she looked across her teams, she saw that the most inclusive environments were also the most innovative. Diverse perspectives flourished where meaning was shared. Resilience grew stronger where people felt valued.

She operationalized this insight immediately:

- NexusNova's Meaning Metrics now included indicators for belonging, equity and voice.

- Managers were trained to analyze meaning data not just by function but intersectionally across identity groups.

- Inclusion councils and meaningful work champions worked side by side – ensuring initiatives reached every team, every geography, every role.

- Most importantly, Zainab elevated stories of meaning from all corners of the business – ensuring that interns, engineers and support reps alike saw their purpose reflected in the culture.

This wasn't just internal. Zainab began speaking at conferences and CEO forums, advocating for the connection between inclusion and meaning. She openly credited Angela's frameworks and Sarah's foundation, while charting a bolder, more inclusive future.

Zainab didn't preach at her peers. She modelled. And that quiet power, paired with the business results, turned doubters into champions.

Giovanni – once the sceptic – became one of her strongest allies. After adopting Zainab's inclusion-enhanced Meaning Metrics at his own company, he saw something remarkable. As culture became more meaning-driven, inclusion increased. Innovation soared. Ideas diversified. Retention improved. He'd had his own awakening – and he credited Zainab for integrating meaningful work with inclusion and seeing impressive results.

'This isn't "soft",' he told a leadership panel. 'This is how the best organizations will win.'

Zainab welcomed the recognition but kept her focus sharp.

'Every person – in every role – deserves meaningful work and an inclusive environment,' she often said.

Not just for knowledge workers. Not just in head offices. Meaning had to reach the factory floor, the call centre, the field. Under Zainab, inclusion wasn't an initiative. It was infrastructure – embedded in the Ecosystem, tracked through data, told through stories and led through behaviour.

And for leaders reading this book, her message is clear: when you embed inclusion into meaning and meaning into inclusion – you don't just build a better workplace. You build a stronger, smarter, more human organization.

The legacy expands

As the months unfolded under Zainab's leadership, NexusNova began to gain widespread recognition.

Articles appeared in industry journals praising its low attrition and high engagement – even during the CEO transition, a moment where culture often wavers. Analysts noted the rare consistency in tone and trust. Zainab, for her part, was clear: this wasn't the result of one person's charisma. It was the outcome of embedded systems, shared ownership and deeply rooted belief.

Other CEOs began reaching out. They weren't just asking about Meaning Metrics or inclusion councils – they were asking about *philosophy*. About leadership. About how to design organizations that endure, not just perform.

Zainab shared freely. She gave credit where it was due to Angela's frameworks, to Sarah's stewardship and to the thousands of NexusNova employees who had turned meaning into practice. At each forum she attended, she championed a new kind of leadership – one where meaning and inclusion weren't the 'nice-to-haves', but the design principles.

And yet, Zainab remained vigilant. She knew that culture was never static – it was a living system. A commitment. A conversation. The workforce was changing. Technology was evolving. Expectations were rising. Rather than see these as threats to stability, she welcomed them as invitations to grow.

'There's no finish line to meaningful work,' she reminded her leadership team.

'And that's what keeps it alive.'

Meanwhile, Sarah observed with satisfaction. She had formally stepped back but remained engaged as a trusted advisor and mentor. She no longer felt the need to be in the room – because the work was being carried, not copied.

She found herself drawn toward a broader mission: helping others start their own meaningful work revolution. She and Angela began quietly advising new CEOs, mentoring change-makers and shaping what would become the wider Lead with Meaning community.

'Stepping back didn't diminish my purpose,' Sarah reflected. 'It amplified it.'

Over dinner one evening, Zainab raised her glass. 'I'm not here to preserve your legacy,' she said to Sarah. 'I'm here to expand it – so every employee, everywhere, feels it for themselves.'

Sarah nodded. And in that moment, she knew it was already happening.

Legacy isn't about what you preserve.

It's about what you empower others to carry forward – and make their own.

It wasn't about her anymore. And that was the point. She hadn't just led with purpose. She had led with meaning.

Your turn to lead

As the final round of applause faded from NexusNova's leadership handover, Sarah stood quietly at the end of the stage. She looked out at the crowd – new leaders, long-standing team members, clients, collaborators – and beyond them, imagined you, the reader, standing there too.

She took one step forward and, in her closing words, spoke not just to the company, but to the world:

'If you're still wondering whether meaning is worth leading with, let the answer be this: the most extraordinary legacy you can leave behind is a workplace where people didn't just perform, they mattered. And they knew it.

You won't just build a better business. You'll know, without doubt, that your leadership made a difference in the lives of real people.

And that's a legacy few can claim.

To the next CEO, to the next changemaker reading this – the baton is now in your hands. You've seen what's possible. Now it's your turn to make it real.'

She wasn't just passing on a philosophy. She was inviting you to carry it forward – in your organization, your team, your decisions, your culture.

Everything you've read in these pages – from the Five Pillars to the Meaning Metrics, to the Ecosystem, the Lead with Meaning playbook and the Legacy Design Loop was built not to inspire from a distance, but to empower action.

You've learned how to diagnose disengagement. You've explored how to design for purpose and equity. You've seen how meaning can fuel inclusion, resilience, performance and innovation. You've witnessed how a movement begins – not with noise, but with intent.

Now it's your turn to decide:

- What kind of workplace do you want to lead?
- What kind of legacy do you want to leave?
- And what would it mean to lead with meaning – not someday, but starting now?

Angela calls it the most crucial decision a leader can make:

'Not what you'll deliver. But what you'll leave behind in others.'

So here, at the edge of this story – as Sarah steps back, Zainab steps forward and the culture continues to evolve – you are invited to step in.

Not because you must. But because, deep down, you want to. Because you've always known leadership could be more. And now, you know how.

The stage is set for your meaningful work revolution.

The next chapter is yours to write.

Final word – a letter to visionary CEOs

Why meaningful work is the future

Dear CEO,

For me, this work began not in theory, but in lived experience. I've led global change initiatives, navigated the tension between purpose and performance and faced the dissonance between values on the wall and the real culture in the room. It was that gap – between what we said and how we behaved – that ignited my search for a better way. The Meaning Over Purpose blueprint is the outcome of that journey.

As you guide your organization through complexity, disruption and accelerated transformation, your greatest strategic opportunity – and your greatest responsibility – lies beyond the boardroom. It's not just about refining your purpose or delivering a new growth plan. It's about designing a culture where people feel a deep, personal connection to their work. A culture where performance is fuelled by meaning.

We stand at an inflection point – a deep shift in what people expect from work and what organizations must deliver if they are to thrive.

Historically, productivity and hierarchy defined work. Employees sought income, stability and upward mobility. Leaders were taught to manage performance through control, metrics and compliance. It was a system that served its time.

But today, that system is breaking down. Across industries and generations, a new set of questions is emerging:

'Why am I here?'

'Does this work matter?'

'Is this a place I want to give my energy to – not just my time?'

They're not just philosophical questions. They're strategic ones. Employees are no longer satisfied with a pay cheque and a purpose statement on the wall. They are seeking alignment. Contribution. Personal resonance. And when they don't feel it, they disengage – quietly, then visibly.

You may feel this already. Your top talent is asking better questions. Your future leaders aren't driven solely by compensation. They want to matter. And they want to know you see that, too.

This is not an HR initiative; it's a CEO-level imperative. Meaning is now the engine of engagement, innovation, retention and performance. It's your greatest opportunity to future-proof your workforce and culture.

Meaningful work is emerging as the defining currency of the future workplace. Organizations that embed meaning into their systems are outperforming peers on innovation, retention and long-term resilience. Those that don't are facing rising attrition, declining engagement and mounting reputational risk – even when their purpose is clear.

This letter is your invitation to lead differently. To move toward a new model of leadership grounded in emotional resonance, psychological insight and cultural sustainability.

We've explored:

- Why meaning is distinct from purpose – and why that distinction matters

- What the world's leading psychologists reveal about how meaning fuels performance

- Five practical strategies to embed meaningful work into your business model at scale

- How courageous, human-centred CEOs are already leading the meaning revolution

The question is no longer *if* you should lead with meaning. The question is: *Will you?*

The psychological foundations of meaning at work

As a psychologist, change leader, consulting leader, and now CEO, I've spent years refining what it takes to embed meaning into organizations of every size. But the insights I share with clients stand on the shoulders of powerful thinkers. What follows is not theory – it's the science of performance through meaning.

As a CEO, it's easy to feel the pressure of performance metrics and strategic delivery. But some of the most powerful tools at your disposal aren't found in your operating model – they're found in psychology. Let's explore what some of the world's leading voices in human motivation can teach us about designing truly meaningful organizations.

Adam Grant: impact drives engagement

Adam Grant's research shows that the most powerful driver of motivation is knowing your work matters to someone else. In one of his most cited studies, call centre employees raised significantly more funds after meeting the beneficiaries of their efforts. One conversation shifted their performance – because it made the impact real.

For CEOs, this is not a soft story. It's a strategic lesson: Impact must be seen, not just implied. You can activate this insight by:

- Sharing customer stories in company-wide meetings
- Connecting back-office teams to front-line feedback
- Reinforcing 'why this matters' in every initiative, not just in values decks

Adam also distinguishes between 'givers' and 'takers'. Giver cultures – those built on generosity, collaboration and contribution – consistently outperform 'taker' cultures. Meaning flourishes when people work in service of something larger than themselves.

Finally, Adam highlights the importance of psychological safety – the freedom to speak up without fear. Without this, meaning withers. As CEO, you set the tone. Your vulnerability becomes permission for others to be human – and to fully show up.

Scott Barry Kaufman: personal growth fuels fulfilment

Scott Barry Kaufman reframes self-actualization not as a luxury, but as a leadership imperative. In *Transcend: The New Science of Self-Actualization*, he urges us to see workplaces as environments for personal growth – not just professional delivery. He also introduces the concept of *transcendence* – the experience of seeing how your growth contributes to something far beyond yourself.

Your employees want more than career progression. They want to:

- Use their strengths
- Grow as people
- Contribute to something that matters to them and the world

This doesn't require a revolution. It requires intentionality:

- Design stretch roles based on strengths, not just gaps
- Create spaces to reflect on team impact, not just output
- Invite employees into purpose-building, not just implementation

When people feel they're growing – and that growth is contributing – resilience soars.

Angela Duckworth: grit is powered by meaning and purpose

Angela Duckworth's work on grit offers a compelling message for CEOs: talent matters. But passion and perseverance matter more. Her research shows that employees who feel their work is meaningful are far more likely to persist through adversity. Grit isn't just about stamina. It's about staying power with purpose.

You can apply this by:

- Linking resilience conversations to meaning, not just productivity
- Celebrating persistence in service of impact, not just high performance

- Modelling your own grit, while sharing the purpose that drives it

In times of change or crisis, meaning is the well people draw from. Your job is to keep that well full.

Susan David: emotional agility emerges from authentic leadership

Susan David's concept of emotional agility is especially relevant for senior leaders. Her research shows that meaning doesn't arise from avoiding difficult emotions, but from navigating them honestly.

Susan encourages leaders to:

- Create space for emotional truth in teams

- Embrace discomfort as data, not disruption

- Model psychological flexibility through your own behaviour

Meaning emerges when people feel they can be human at work – and still succeed. For CEOs, this is not about being soft. It's about being real. Because realness builds trust and trust fuels engagement. Together, these psychological insights form a leadership toolkit:

- Adam Grant teaches us that impact must be visible

- Scott Barry Kaufman reminds us of that personal growth drives contribution

- Angela Duckworth shows that grit is sustained by meaning

- Susan David challenges us to lead with emotional depth

These are not tangential to performance. They are the *drivers* of performance.

In our work, we've seen this clearly: teams that report high meaning scores bounce back faster and outperform even during prolonged change cycles.

Five practical actions for CEOs to embed meaning

You don't need a culture overhaul to start leading with meaning.

But you do need to lead *intentionally* – weaving meaning into the rhythms of leadership, the structures of your systems and the emotional tone of your organization.

Here are five strategic actions you can take right now to begin.

1. Differentiate purpose from meaning – and communicate both

Purpose is your organizational north star. It's 'why'. Meaning is each person's 'why me'. If you are only communicating the first, you are only doing half the job.

Many organizations confuse the two – but they are not the same. Your purpose may be to revolutionize sustainability, democratize technology or serve vulnerable communities. But if your employees don't feel how their specific role contributes, meaning never takes root.

As CEO:

- Make this distinction clear in internal messaging

- Use the Purpose-to-Meaning Gap framework to start conversations

- Ask leaders to connect purpose to role-level meaning in every team update

When people can say, 'I understand the purpose – and I know why my work matters in that,' everything changes.

2. Create and celebrate meaningful moments

Meaning is not found in mission statements. It is built through everyday rituals, conversations and recognition.

As CEO:

- Start meetings with 'Why this matters' – not just what's on the agenda

- Highlight stories of purpose, impact or grit at all-hands or in newsletters

- Celebrate not just outcomes, but the values lived along the way

Leaders can actively use the Lead with Meaning playbook habit of 'Framing the Why' – embedding context and human connection into the routine flow of work.

Meaning needs to be felt. The most powerful way to embed it is through consistent, emotionally resonant storytelling. These don't need to be polished. They need to be real.

3. Foster authentic conversations about meaning

Culture is created in the quality of conversation. Make meaning a leadership topic – not a wellbeing sideline. Meaningful work can't be assumed.

Ask your people:

- 'Where do you find meaning in your role?'

- 'What gives you energy here?'

- 'Where are we falling short of what we say we stand for?'

These conversations are powerful – and revealing. But they require psychological safety.

As CEO, you can model this by:

- Inviting feedback and admitting where meaning has been missed

- Sharing your own 'why' – not the press release version, but the human one

- Encouraging managers to explore meaning with their teams regularly

Employees who can speak about meaning are more engaged, more loyal and more likely to lead others.

4. Measure meaning, not just engagement

Engagement tells you *what* people feel. Meaning tells you *why* they feel it.

If you're only measuring engagement, you're measuring after the fact. Meaning is what drives it – and Meaning Metrics can track it early, deeply and often.

Start measuring:

- Alignment (do employees feel their work fits their values?)
- Growth (are they developing in ways that matter?)
- Connection (do they feel seen, safe and part of something?)
- Resonance (does their work feel worthwhile?)

This is the basis of Meaning Metrics. Whether you build your own or use ours, the key is this: what gets measured gets managed. But what gets *felt* gets remembered.

5. Develop leaders who lead with meaning

Your culture is not your values. Your culture is how your leaders behave – especially when it's hard.

Equip them to:

- Frame work with why, not just deliverables
- Recognize effort and impact, not just output
- Lead with emotional agility and human-centred practices
- Encourage autonomy, reflection and purpose in conversations
- Use the Lead with Meaning playbook to turn values into action

Great leadership now requires emotional literacy, clarity of purpose and the ability to build meaning in motion. Train for that – and your culture will hold, even through pressure.

These five actions are culture design tools. They won't just improve morale. They will:

- Reduce attrition

- Boost resilience

- Improve innovation

- Deepen commitment

- Strengthen the emotional contract between your organization and your people

Because meaning isn't a side effect of great leadership. It's the *outcome* of it.

Leading the meaning revolution – A CEO call to action

We are living through a defining moment – not just in business, but in leadership.

For decades, CEOs have been taught to lead through performance, precision and growth. And yes, those things still matter but they are no longer enough. The next frontier isn't faster. It's *deeper*.

The future will belong to leaders who build organizations where meaning drives performance – not just purpose on paper.

The evidence is clear:

- Companies that embed meaningful work experience higher innovation, stronger engagement and greater resilience

- Employees who find their work meaningful are more loyal, more creative and more willing to go the extra mile

- Cultures built on meaning don't just retain talent – they multiply it

This is your moment. As CEO, you already know how to drive performance. Now it's time to elevate it – through meaning. And the leaders who embrace this truth are already shaping the future.

Look at Satya Nadella at Microsoft – who rebuilt an entire company culture by replacing control with curiosity and rehumanizing leadership. Or Yvon Chouinard at Patagonia – who embedded meaning through values, service and activism, long before it was fashionable.

These are not feel-good stories. They are performance stories. Because when people believe in their work, they *give* more – and stay longer.

So, here's your invitation – and your challenge:

Step into a new model of leadership. Not one defined by control, charisma or compliance, but one defined by:

- Courage – to ask what's really driving disengagement

- Clarity – to separate purpose from meaning and lead both

- Empathy – to hear what your people need and act on it

- Integrity – to measure what matters, not just what's easy

- Vision – to build a legacy that outlasts your tenure

This is what it means to lead the meaning revolution.

To turn culture into strategy, metrics into momentum, values into velocity and your leadership into legacy. And while it starts with you, it will not end with you. Because once meaning is embedded, it doesn't need to be chased. It carries itself.

You've seen the frameworks. You've read the research. You've walked alongside Sarah, Zainab and Giovanni as they discovered what it really means to lead with meaning.

Now it's your turn. The world doesn't need another performance-driven CEO. It needs a meaning-driven one.

And if you've read this far, I suspect that's who you are.

Taking the next step – lead with meaning

If this chapter has challenged your thinking – good. If it has affirmed your vision – better. But now, it's time to act.

At The Centre for Meaningful Work, we've spent years researching, testing and refining the models you've read about in this book: the Five Pillars of Meaningful Work, the Meaningful Work Ecosystem, Meaning Metrics and the Lead with Meaning playbook. These aren't concepts, they're practical tools. And they work.

We've seen them work across industries, cultures and leadership styles. We've helped leaders embed them into their organizations and we've watched those cultures thrive – not just in engagement scores, but in innovation, resilience and lasting emotional commitment.

It has been the honour of my life's work to help leaders build meaning. I write this knowing the journey is challenging but wholeheartedly believing in you, the reader, to carry this forward.

We'd be honoured to help you. Whether you're looking to:

- Coach your executive team on meaning-based leadership
- Equip your managers with tools for autonomy, connection and impact
- Upskill your HR teams, internal consultants or coaches in Own Your Meaning for individuals or the Lead with Meaning leadership playbook
- Redesign your cultural architecture
- Or shape your personal leadership legacy around lasting, human impact…

… we're here.

Through bespoke executive coaching, enterprise-wide consulting and our Lead with Meaning programmes, we partner with CEOs and senior teams.

When you lead with meaning, you do more than inspire your people. You build a company they want to belong to, you create a culture they'll fight to protect, and you leave behind something greater than results: you leave a workplace where people didn't just work – they mattered.

So, if this message resonates – let's begin a conversation. Visit us at www.thecentreformeaningfulwork.com

The future of meaningful work is already underway. Let's make it extraordinary. With purpose, clarity and meaning,

So, I ask you, what is one thing you will do differently on Monday to start closing the meaning gap in your organization?

Angela Rixon

CEO, The Centre for Meaningful Work

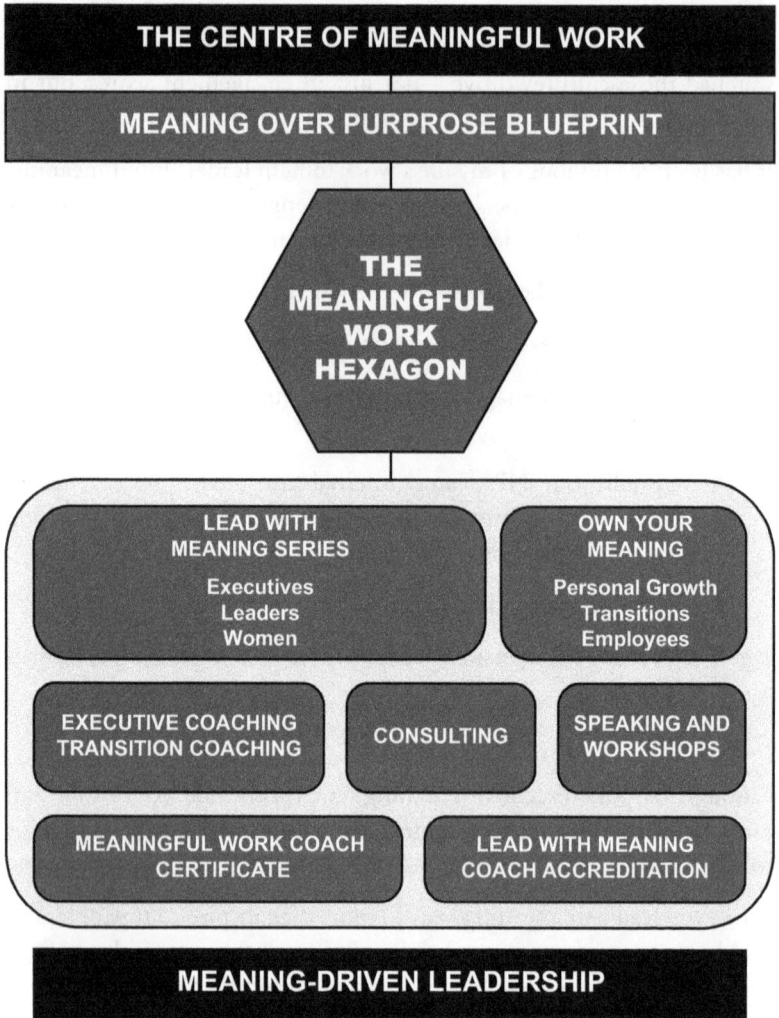

Figure 18: The Centre for Meaningful Work is the home of the Meaning Over Purpose blueprint, a proven system for building resilient, high-performing cultures where people thrive. Through our frameworks, programmes and partnerships, we support leaders, employees, coaches and organizations in designing meaningful work that lasts.

Appendices

Practical tools for embedding meaning

In these appendices, you will find actionable assessments, audits and frameworks to help you evaluate and implement meaningful work principles in your context. Each tool aligns with concepts from the chapters, providing a bridge from insight to action. Use them to diagnose where you stand and to spark strategic conversations with your team. Adapt them freely to fit your organization's needs.

Each of the tools – from the organizational audits to individual and team checkups – is designed to make meaning a tangible topic you can work on. Think of them as part of your meaningful work toolkit. By using these diagnostics, you signal to everyone that meaningful work is not just talk – it's something you measure, discuss and actively cultivate (just like any other key metric). This drives home the cultural message.

Each tool is described in the following pages and can be downloaded at https://thecentreformeaningfulwork.com.

Appendix 1 – Meaning Gap Self-Diagnostic

Identify where purpose is felt and where meaning may be missing in your current role or organization.

https://thecentreformeaningfulwork.com/meaninggap

Appendix 2 – Cultural Embedding Audit

Assess how well meaningful work is embedded in your systems, rituals, leadership practices and environment.

https://thecentreformeaningfulwork.com/cultureaudit

Appendix 3 – Personal Meaning Inventory

Explore your individual drivers of meaning, aligned to values, growth, impact and connection.

https://thecentreformeaningfulwork.com/personalmeaning

Appendix 4 – Team Meaningfulness Health Check

Use this team-based reflection to surface what's helping and hindering meaningful work in your shared environment.

https://thecentreformeaningfulwork.com/teamcheck

These tools are designed to be used flexibly: on your own, in workshops, in coaching conversations, or as part of broader organizational initiatives. Whether you're a CEO, team leader or individual contributor, they're here to help you start where you are, and lead with meaning from there.

Illustration references

As you implement changes, refer to the Meaningful Work Hexagon (Figure 3) to ensure you're touching on all facets (purpose, personal, leadership, culture, impact, systems) in your improvement plans. Use the Purpose-to-Meaning Gap (Figure 1) diagram to explain to colleagues why these efforts matter (bridging that gap improves engagement and performance). And consider the Five Pillars (Figure 8) diagram when brainstorming solutions (Are we giving the team more Autonomy? Are we fostering Connection?) as needed based on the gaps identified. Aligning practical actions with those frameworks will keep your efforts holistic and effective.

Lastly, lead by example. Use these tools on yourself and your teams openly. Share what you learned, even if some of it is critical. Showing vulnerability and commitment to improvement will encourage others to do the same. As a leader, when you openly say, for instance, 'Our self-assessment showed we're not so great at celebrating meaningful wins. I take that to heart and here's what I propose we do…,' you create a ripple of trust and accountability.

These appendices close the book but ideally open a new set of conversations and actions in your organization. Leadership is an ongoing journey of learning and adapting. Keep striving, keep measuring and keep meaning at the forefront of your leadership practice.

Congratulations on taking these steps – you are moving from understanding Meaning Over Purpose to living it. The tools and insights in this book, combined with your courage and dedication, will help you create not just success, but significance. That is the ultimate legacy of a great leader. Good luck!

If you would like help to educate, design, train or implement meaningful work in your organization, please contact The Centre for Meaningful Work at www.thecentreformeaningfulwork.com

Appendix 1
Meaning Gap Self-diagnostic Tool

Purpose

Gauge the extent to which your organization currently provides meaningful work experiences. This quick survey helps identify meaning gaps – areas where there is misalignment between stated purpose/values and employees' daily experiences.

How to use

Leaders can take this individually or administer it to their teams and aggregate results. Rate your organization on each statement from 1 (not true) to 5 (very true). Be brutally honest – the goal is to uncover truths.

1. Our employees understand and can articulate why their work matters beyond financial metrics. (Do people see the real-world impact or bigger purpose of their tasks?)

2. Leadership consistently communicates the broader impact of our work, beyond profits and short-term goals. (Do leaders talk about mission, values, stakeholder impact regularly?)

3. We have frequent, authentic conversations about personal and collective meaning at work. (Are topics like purpose, fulfilment or the 'why' part of normal discourse or are they taboo?)

4. Employees regularly see how their specific roles contribute to the company's mission and values. (Is the line of sight clear from each desk to the mission statement?)

5. Leaders at all levels visibly align their actions with our stated values and purpose. (Do middle managers 'walk the talk' or is there values hypocrisy?)

6. Employees have opportunities to connect their personal passions and values with their day-to-day work. (Through stretch assignments, volunteering, project choice, etc.)

7. We regularly share and celebrate stories of employees making a meaningful impact. (Are narratives of meaning part of meetings, newsletters, town halls?)

8. Employees feel comfortable openly discussing what feels meaningful – or meaningless – in their roles. (Is there psychological safety to give feedback if work feels pointless or value misaligned?)

Scoring

Add up the ratings.

- 32–40: Excellent! You are actively closing the meaning gap. Leverage this strength and keep refining – meaning is a moving target.

- 24–31: Good, but there is room to deepen meaningful work practices. Identify the lower-scoring areas and focus there for improvement (e.g., if storytelling is lacking, start there).

- 16–23: Noticeable meaning gap – strategic action is recommended. Multiple aspects need work. Consider a comprehensive initiative (you likely have many disengaged folks yearning for more meaning).

- Below 16: Critical meaning gap – urgent leadership attention is needed. This is showing up in low engagement or high turnover. It's time to treat meaningful work as a top strategic priority (reread this book with your exec team and formulate an action plan).

Next steps

Reflect on any statements where you scored 3 or below. These are gaps to address. For each, brainstorm two immediate actions you as a leader can take. For example, if statement 5 (leader alignment) was low, one action might be to establish an internal 'values audit' where employees rate leadership behaviours and leaders then address missteps openly. Consider sharing the overall results with your senior leadership team to build urgency. You could even facilitate a discussion: 'Here's where we think we stand on providing meaningful work – where can we do better?' Use this tool periodically (every 6–12 months) to track progress as you implement changes.

This diagnostic aligns with concepts from Chapters 1 and 2 on assessing the current state of meaning in your workplace.

Appendix 2
Meaningful Work Cultural Embedding Audit

Purpose

A self-assessment for CEOs and senior leaders to evaluate how deeply meaningful work is structurally embedded in the organization. It goes beyond individual feelings to examine policies, processes and systems.

How to use

Rate each statement on the extent you agree (1 = strongly disagree, 5 = strongly agree). This audit focuses on institutionalization – the 'hard wiring' discussed in Chapter 12.

1. Our hiring, onboarding and promotion processes explicitly include meaningful work criteria (e.g., aligning values, purpose-fit).

2. Leaders consistently reinforce meaningful work through daily routines and behaviours (gratitude, storytelling, connecting tasks to purpose).

3. HR and performance management systems evaluate and reward meaningful contributions, not just task outputs.

4. We have formal programs for leadership development that emphasize emotional intelligence, coaching and purpose-driven management.

5. There are structured opportunities (rituals, meetings) for employees to reflect on and share what makes their work meaningful.

6. Psychological safety is actively cultivated – e.g., managers are trained to solicit input and handle failure in a learning-oriented way.

7. Innovation processes involve employees at all levels and encourage diverse perspectives (indicating inclusive meaning-making).

8. We regularly measure culture and meaning (through surveys, Meaning Metrics dashboards) and act transparently on the results.

9. Stories of meaningful impact (especially involving customers or community) are collected and disseminated internally to reinforce purpose.

10. Our succession plans prioritize candidates' commitment to our cultural values and ability to lead with meaning and inclusion.

Reflection

High scores (4–5) across these statements confirm that meaningful work is baked into your company's architecture – fantastic. Any statement scoring 3 or below flags an area to integrate meaning more deeply. For instance, if #3 is low (systems don't reward meaningful contributions), you might revamp performance reviews to include categories like collaboration, living the values, mentoring others (and train managers on how to evaluate these fairly). If #8 is low (not measuring), consider implementing an annual 'meaningfulness index' or adding questions to your engagement survey like 'I find my work meaningful', and then use that data.

This audit pairs with Chapter 12's Steps 1 and 3 in legacy building – institutionalizing values and rituals. The more 'yes' answers there are here, the more self-sustaining your culture will be.

Next steps

For each statement rated low, identify one structural change to make in the next quarter. Small changes can have big effects (e.g., adding a 5-minute 'mission moment' in weekly team meetings could significantly boost #2 over time). Revisit this audit annually to ensure continuous improvement. Remember, culture change is a marathon, not a sprint – but every structural tweak moves you closer to a workplace where meaning thrives.

Appendix 3
Personal Meaningful
Work Inventory

Purpose

Adapted for leaders and individual contributors alike, this tool helps an individual assess their own experience of meaningful work. It can highlight where you personally derive meaning and where you might need to seek or create more.

To reflect on and increase your personal sense of meaning in your work. Leaders should do this for themselves (a leader who finds their own work meaningful is far more effective) and can also share it with team members as a development exercise.

How to use

Rate the extent you agree with each statement about your work (1 = not at all, 5 = completely true):

1. I understand how my work contributes to something larger (the team's goals, the company mission or societal needs).

2. My work aligns with my personal values and the things I care about in life. I feel I'm working for a cause or principle that matters to me.

3. I see a positive impact from my work on others (colleagues, customers or the community). Even if it is small, I see I made a difference.

4. My job allows me to use and develop my strengths and talents. I have a chance to experience Mastery and growth, rather than feeling my potential is wasted.

5. I often experience a sense of connection or belonging at work. I feel part of a community or team; I'm not just isolated.

6. I feel that my work helps me become a better person or learn about myself. Work challenges me in a way that contributes to personal growth or self-understanding.

7. There is a strong sense of purpose in my day-to-day tasks. I rarely question 'why am I doing this?' – the answer is usually clear.

8. I would still choose this work if I had other options that paid similar. (This gauges intrinsic motivation – if it's purely extrinsic, meaning is likely to be low.)

9. When I describe my job to others, I feel proud of not just what I do, but *why* I do it. I can articulate the meaning of my work.

10. If I left this job, I would miss the sense of purpose it gives me. (Would the meaning be a major thing, beyond people or perks?)

Reflection

There are no definitive scores here, but generally, lots of 4s and 5s indicate you currently find strong meaning in work. If you have many 1s or 2s, it's a sign of a significant meaning gap for you personally – potentially a risk factor for disengagement or burnout. For mid-scores, it's an opportunity to identify where to seek improvement.

Look at any statements you rated low (1–3). These represent facets of meaningful work that you might be lacking, for example, if #5 (connection) is low, perhaps you feel lonely at work – you could focus on building more relationships or teamwork. If #2 (values alignment) is low, perhaps something about the work clashes with your personal ideals – that may need addressing, either by changing how you work or considering a role shift if possible. If #6 (personal growth) is low, seek stretch projects or learning opportunities that inject more personal development into your routine.

As a leader, encourage your team members to reflect on these questions. It might even be eye-opening to discuss in a one-on-one: ask them what gives them the most meaning and what feels meaningless. Those conversations can guide job crafting – small changes to better align roles with passions and strengths.

Next steps

Choose one statement where you scored yourself lowest and brainstorm with a mentor or colleague one change to improve that area. For example, low on 'positive impact on others'? Consider volunteering for a corporate social responsibility initiative or find ways to get direct feedback from end-users of your work – seeing how your output helps someone can boost perceived impact. Low on 'using my strengths'? Speak with your manager about tasks you excel at and enjoy and try to do more of those.

Remember, meaningful work is partly what the organization provides and partly what you make of it. This inventory empowers you to take charge of the latter. Sometimes a conversation, a shift in perspective or a proactive change can transform how you experience your job, even if the job itself doesn't change.

This tool resonates with Chapter 3 on personal drivers of meaning and Chapter 5 on job re-crafting. It can also be used in workshops for employee development.

Appendix 4
Team Meaningfulness
Health Check

Purpose

To help team leaders assess the climate of meaning within a team. A team could be a department, project group or business unit. The focus here is on the collective experience – do we as a team feel our work is meaningful and that we work together meaningfully?

How to use

As a team leader, you could use this as a pulse survey (formal or informal) with your team members or as a discussion framework in a team meeting. Rate or discuss each item:

1. Our team has a clear understanding of how our goals support the organization's mission. (Clarity of why the team exists and why it matters)

2. Team members regularly discuss the impact of our work, not just the output. (We talk about how our work benefits others, not only task metrics)

3. Within the team, we acknowledge each other's contributions and express gratitude frequently. (This indicates a culture where people feel valued – ties to Connection and Impact)

4. We have shared values or a team mantra that gives us a sense of purpose in how we work together. (e.g., 'We put customers first' or 'Quality above all' – something that bonds the team)

5. Everyone on the team has opportunities to use their strengths and grow. (No one feels stuck just doing grunt work)

6. The team environment is inclusive – diverse viewpoints are welcomed and everyone feels they belong. (Psychological safety and inclusion is crucial for meaning)

7. When setbacks occur, we discuss what we learned and how it connects to our bigger purpose, rather than just assigning blame. (Indicates resilience and keeping sight of meaning even under stress)

8. Team celebrations highlight meaningful achievements rather than only hitting targets. (e.g., how we helped a client)

9. Communication in our team often circles back to 'why we do this'. (Keeping purpose front and centre)

10. If given the choice, most of us would want to keep working together because there's a special sense of mission or camaraderie here. (This is a gut-check: do people feel this team is about more than just a salary?)

Reflection

If you find several 'no' or low ratings, the team might be lacking in collective meaning. The leader can facilitate improvements: for instance, if #1 or #2 is weak (lack of connection to mission), bring that context into meetings more often – remind the team who the end-user is, share customer feedback or big-picture updates. If #6 is an issue (inclusion), address any cliques or dynamics that marginalize members; rotate roles or ensure equal voice in discussions. If #3 is low (lack of gratitude), start modelling it – call out team members' good work in meetings and encourage peer recognition.

A high-functioning, meaningful team often has its own subculture of purpose and support that aligns with the larger company culture. These teams are gold – they often outperform because members are engaged and have each other's backs.

Next steps

Discuss as a team any statements that were rated low or had disagreement. Ask the team: *What could we do to improve in this area?* Often the best ideas come from the team members themselves – after all, it's *their* experience. Perhaps suggest starting meetings with a quick story of impact or instituting a 'shout-out' section in the team newsletter or having a quarterly offsite to reconnect with purpose. Be open to ideas.

This health check should not be one-and-done. Revisit it periodically. Teams evolve as new people join or projects change. Keeping a pulse on team meaningfulness will help you maintain high morale and performance. It turns abstract concepts into conversational, manageable topics.

References

Amabile, T.M. and Kramer, S.J. (2011). 'The Power of Small Wins', *Harvard Business Review*, May. Available at: https://hbr.org/2011/05/the-power-of-small-wins (Accessed: 7 April 2025).

Avey, J.B., Wernsing, T.S. and Luthans, F. (2008). 'Can positive employees help positive organizational change? Impact of psychological capital and emotions on relevant attitudes and behaviors', *Journal of Applied Behavioral Science*, 44(1), pp. 48–70. https://doi.org/10.1177/0021886307311470

Avolio, B.J. and Gardner, W.L. (2005). 'Authentic Leadership Development: Getting to the Root of Positive Forms of Leadership', *Leadership Quarterly*, 16(3), pp. 315–338.

Bailey, C. and Madden, A. (2016). 'What Makes Work Meaningful – or Meaningless', *MIT Sloan Management Review*, 57(4), pp. 53–61.

Bandura, A. (1986). *Social Foundations of Thought and Action: A Social Cognitive Theory*. Englewood Cliffs, NJ: Prentice-Hall.

Bartlett, C.A. and Ghoshal, S. (1998). *Managing Across Borders: The Transnational Solution*. 2nd edn. Boston: Harvard Business School Press.

Baumeister, R.F. (1991). *Meanings of Life*. New York: Guilford Press.

Beckhard, R. and Harris, R.T. (1987). *Organizational Transitions: Managing Complex Change*. 2nd edn. Reading, MA: Addison-Wesley.

Beer, M., Finnström, M. and Schrader, D. (2016). 'Why leadership training fails – and what to do about it', *Harvard Business Review*, October. Available at: https://hbr.org/2016/10/why-leadership-training-fails-and-what-to-do-about-it

Bloom, P. (2018). 'The Origins of Meaning in Life and Work'. *Yale Insights*. Available at: https://insights.som.yale.edu (Accessed: 7 April 2025).

Bridges, W. (2009). *Managing Transitions: Making the Most of Change*. 3rd edn. Philadelphia: Da Capo Press.

Bronfenbrenner, U. (1977). 'Toward an Experimental Ecology of Human Development', *American Psychologist*, 32(7), pp. 513–531.

Brown, B. (2012). *Daring Greatly: How the Courage to Be Vulnerable Transforms the Way We Live, Love, Parent and Lead*. New York: Gotham Books.

Brown, B. (2018). *Dare to Lead: Brave Work. Tough Conversations. Whole Hearts*. New York: Random House.

Bunderson, J.S. and Thompson, J.A. (2009). 'The Call of the Wild: Zookeepers, Callings and the Double-Edged Sword of Deeply Meaningful Work', *Administrative Science Quarterly*, 54(1), pp. 32–57.

Cameron, E. and Green, M. (2015). *Making Sense of Change Management*. 4th edn. London: Kogan Page.

Cameron, K.S., Bright, D. and Caza, A. (2011). 'Positive Practices in the Workplace: Impact on Team Climate and Organizational Performance', *Journal of Applied Behavioral Science*, 47(3), pp. 266–308.

Cameron, K.S. and Spreitzer, G.M. (eds.) (2012). *The Oxford Handbook of Positive Organizational Scholarship*. Oxford: Oxford University Press.

Chatman, J.A. and O'Reilly, C.A. (2016). 'Paradigm Lost: Reinvigorating the Study of Organizational Culture', *Research in Organizational Behavior*, 36, pp. 199–224.

Collins, J. (2005). 'Level 5 Leadership: The Triumph of Humility and Fierce Resolve', *Harvard Business Review*, July–August. Available at: https://hbr.org/2005/07/level-5-leadership (Accessed: 7 April 2025).

Collins, J.C. and Porras, J.I. (1994). *Built to Last: Successful Habits of Visionary Companies*. New York: HarperBusiness.

Collins, J.C. and Porras, J.I. (1997). 'Building Your Company's Vision', *Harvard Business Review*, September–October. Available at: https://hbr.org/1996/09/building-your-companys-vision (Accessed: 7 April 2025).

Covey, S.R. (2004). *The 8th Habit: From Effectiveness to Greatness*. New York: Free Press.

Cross, R. and Parker, A. (2004). *The Hidden Power of Social Networks: Understanding How Work Really Gets Done in Organizations*. Boston, MA: Harvard Business Review Press.

Crum, A.J., Salovey, P. and Achor, S. (2013). 'Rethinking Stress: The Role of Mindsets in Determining the Stress Response', *Journal of Personality and Social Psychology*, 104(4), pp. 716–733.

Csikszentmihalyi, M. (1990). *Flow: The Psychology of Optimal Experience*. New York: Harper & Row.

Deci, E.L. and Ryan, R.M. (2000). 'The "What" and "Why" of Goal Pursuits: Human Needs and the Self-Determination of Behavior', *Psychological Inquiry*, 11(4), pp. 227–268.

Deloitte. (2016). *Culture: Prime Ingredient in Employee Success*. Deloitte Insights. Available at: www2.deloitte.com (Accessed: 7 April 2025).

Deloitte. (2019). *The Economics of Purpose: How Purpose Drives Profit and Performance*. Deloitte Insights. Available at: www2.deloitte.com (Accessed: 7 April 2025).

Deloitte. (2020). 2020 Global Human Capital Trends: Delivering results with Oracle HCM Cloud. Deloitte. Available at: https://www.deloitte.com/global/en/alliances/oracle/about/global-human-capital-trends-delivering-results-with-oracle-hcm-cloud.html (Accessed: 10 July 2025).

Deloitte. (2021). 2021 Deloitte Global Millennial and Gen Z Survey. Deloitte Insights. Available at: ww2.deloitte.com/global/en/pages/about-deloitte/articles/millennialsurvey.html (Accessed: 1 June 2025).

Deloitte. (2022). 2022 Deloitte Global Human Capital Trends Report: The Worker–Employer Relationship Disrupted. Deloitte Insights. Available at: www2.deloitte.com/insights/us/en/focus/human-capital-trends/2022.html (Accessed: 1 June 2025).

Deloitte. (2023). 2023 Global Human Capital Trends: New Fundamentals for a Boundaryless World. Deloitte Insights. Available at: www2.deloitte.com/us/en/insights/focus/human-capital-trends/2023.html (Accessed: 1 June 2025).

Deloitte. (2024). 2024 Deloitte Global Millennial and Gen Z Survey. Deloitte Insights. Available at: www2.deloitte.com/global/en/pages/about-deloitte/articles/millennialsurvey.html (Accessed: 1 June 2025).

Denison, D.R. (1990). *Corporate Culture and Organizational Effectiveness*. New York: Wiley.

Dik, B.J. and Duffy, R.D. (2009). 'Calling and Vocation at Work: Definitions and Prospects for Research and Practice', *The Counseling Psychologist*, 37(3), pp. 424–450.

Dik, B.J., Byrne, Z.S. and Steger, M.F. (eds.) (2013). *Purpose and Meaning in the Workplace*. Washington, DC: American Psychological Association.

Dutton, J.E., Roberts, L.M. and Bednar, J.S. (2010). 'Pathways for positive identity construction at work: Four types of positive identity and the building of social resources', *Academy of Management Review*, 35(2), pp. 265–293. Available at: https://doi.org/10.5465/amr.35.2.zok265

Dweck, C.S. (2006). *Mindset: The New Psychology of Success*. New York: Random House.

Economic Times, The (2024). 'Microsoft CEO Satya Nadella caps a decade of change and tremendous growth.' Available at: https://economictimes.indiatimes.com/tech/technology/microsoft-ceo-satya-nadella-caps-a-decade-of-change-and-tremendous-growth/articleshow/107385792.cms (Accessed: 10 July 2025).

Edmans, A. (2012). 'The Link Between Job Satisfaction and Firm Value, With Implications for Corporate Social Responsibility', *Academy of Management Perspectives*, 26(4), pp. 1–19.

Edmondson, A.C. (1999). 'Psychological Safety and Learning Behavior in Work Teams', *Administrative Science Quarterly*, 44(2), pp. 350–383.

Edmondson, A.C. and Lei, Z. (2014). 'Psychological Safety: The History, Renaissance and Future of an Interpersonal Construct', *Annual Review of Organizational Psychology and Organizational Behavior*, 1(1), pp. 23–43.

Erikson, E.H. (1959). *Identity and the Life Cycle*. New York: International Universities Press.

Fisher, C.D. (2010). 'Happiness at Work', *International Journal of Management Reviews*, 12(4), pp. 384–412.

Folger, R. and Skarlicki, D.P. (1999). 'Unfairness and Resistance to Change: Hardship as Mistreatment', *Journal of Organizational Change Management*, 12(1), pp. 35–50.

Frankl, V.E. (1959). *Man's Search for Meaning*. Boston: Beacon Press.

Frederick, J. (2021). 'Purpose-Oriented Workers and the Changing Experience of Work', WorqIQ. Available at: https://worqiq.com/2017/10/purpose-oriented-workers-experience-work/ (Accessed: 1 June 2025).

Gallup. (2019). State of the American Workplace Report. Washington, DC: Gallup. Available at: www.gallup.com/workplace/257578/state-american-workplace-report-2019.aspx (Accessed: 1 June 2025).

Gallup. (2020). *Employee Engagement and Wellbeing During COVID-19: The 2020 Update*. Washington, DC: Gallup.

Gallup. (2021). State of the Global Workplace: 2021 Report. Washington, DC: Gallup. Available at: www.gallup.com/workplace/349484/state-of-the-global-workplace-2021.aspx (Accessed: 1 June 2025).

Gallup. (2022). State of the Global Workplace: 2022 Report. Washington, DC: Gallup. Available at: www.gallup.com/workplace/393197/state-global-work place-2022.aspx (Accessed: 1 June 2025).

Gallup. (2023). State of the Global Workplace: 2023 Report. Washington, DC: Gallup. Available at: www.gallup.com/workplace/505654/state-of-the-global-workplace-2023.aspx (Accessed: 1 June 2025).

Gallup. (2024). State of the Global Workplace: 2024 Report. Washington, DC: Gallup. Available at: www.gallup.com/workplace/2024-global-report.aspx (Accessed: 1 June 2025).

Gartner (2022a). 'Revitalizing culture in the world of hybrid work,' *Harvard Business Review*, November–December. Available at: https://hbr.org/2022/11/revitalizing-culture-in-the-world-of-hybrid-work (Accessed: 22 June 2025).

Gartner (2022b). 'Think hybrid work doesn't work? The data disagrees.' Gartner. Available at: https://www.gartner.com/en/articles/think-hybrid-work-doesn-t-work-the-data-disagrees (Accessed: 22 June 2025).

Gartner (2022c). 'People feel disconnected from company culture. But is hybrid work the problem?,' *HR Dive*, 23 May. Available at: https://www.hrdive.com/news/people-feel-disconnected-from-company-culture-but-is-hybrid-work-the-problem/624178/ (Accessed: 22 June 2025).

Gartner (2024). 'Gartner HR research: 41% of HR leaders say hybrid work is weakening cultural connection,' *Gartner Research Brief*, 15 February. Available at: https://www.gartner.com/en/newsroom (Accessed: 22 June 2025).

George, B. (2003). *Authentic Leadership: Rediscovering the Secrets to Creating Lasting Value*. San Francisco: Jossey-Bass.

Gibson, William, attributed quote: 'The future is already here – it's just not evenly distributed.'

Goleman, D. (1998). 'What Makes a Leader?', *Harvard Business Review*, November–December. Available at: https://hbr.org/1998/11/what-makes-a-leader (Accessed: 7 April 2025).

Grant, A.M. (2007). 'Relational Job Design and the Motivation to Make a Prosocial Difference', *Academy of Management Review*, 32(2), pp. 393–417.

Grant, A.M. (2013). *Give and Take: A Revolutionary Approach to Success*. New York: Viking.

Great Place to Work. (2022). 'The Business Case for a High-Trust Culture'. Great Place to Work. Available at: www.greatplacetowork.com/resources/reports/the-business-case-for-a-high-trust-culture (Accessed: 1 June 2025).

Greenleaf, R.K. (1977). *Servant Leadership: A Journey into the Nature of Legitimate Power and Greatness*. New York: Paulist Press.

Hackman, J.R. and Oldham, G.R. (1976). 'Motivation through the Design of Work: Test of a Theory', *Organizational Behavior and Human Performance*, 16(2), pp. 250–279.

Hall, D.T. and Chandler, D.E. (2005). 'Psychological success: When the career is a calling', *Journal of Organizational Behavior*, 26(2), pp. 155–176. https://doi.org/10.1002/job.301

Hargreaves, A. and Fink, D. (2006). *Sustainable Leadership*. San Francisco: Jossey-Bass.

Harter, J.K., Schmidt, F.L. and Keyes, C.L.M. (2003). 'Well-Being in the Workplace and Its Relationship to Business Outcomes', *Gallup Research Journal*, 9(3), pp. 205–221.

Harvard Business Review Analytic Services. (2015). 'The Impact of Employee Engagement on Performance', *Harvard Business Review*. Available at: https://hbr.org/resources/pdfs/comm/achievers/hbr_impact_employ_engagement.pdf (Accessed: 1 June 2025).

Hastings, R. and Meyer, E. (2020). *No Rules Rules: Netflix and the Culture of Reinvention*. London: Virgin Books.

Heifetz, R.A. and Linsky, M. (2002). *Leadership on the Line*. Boston: Harvard Business School Press.

Hesselbein, F. and Goldsmith, M. (eds.) (2006). *The Leader of the Future 2: Visions, Strategies and Practices for the New Era*. San Francisco: Jossey-Bass.

Higgins, J.M. (2005). 'The Eight "S"s of Successful Strategy Execution', *Journal of Change Management*, 5(1), pp. 3–13. https://doi.org/10.1080/14697010500036064

Hoffman, R., Casnocha, B. and Yeh, C. (2014). *The Alliance: Managing Talent in the Networked Age*. Boston, MA: Harvard Business Review Press.

Hsieh, T. (2010). *Delivering Happiness: A Path to Profits, Passion and Purpose*. New York: Business Plus.

Humphrey, R.H., Ashkanasy, N.M. and Mahoney, J.M. (2015). 'The bright side of emotional labor', *Journal of Organizational Behavior*, 36(6), pp. 749–769. https://doi.org/10.1002/job.2019

Ibarra, H. (2003). Working Identity: Unconventional Strategies for Reinventing Your Career. Boston, MA: Harvard Business School Press.

IBM. (2021). 'The Employee Experience Index: Key Drivers of Engagement in Hybrid Workplaces'. Armonk, NY: IBM Institute for Business Value.

Kahn, W.A. (1990). 'Psychological conditions of personal engagement and disengagement at work', *Academy of Management Journal*, 33(4), pp. 692–724. https://doi.org/10.5465/256287

Kahn, W.A. (1992). 'To be fully there: Psychological presence at work', *Human Relations*, 45(4), pp. 321–349. https://doi.org/10.1177/001872679204500402

Kaplan, R.S. and Norton, D.P. (1996). *The Balanced Scorecard: Translating Strategy into Action*. Boston: Harvard Business School Press.

Kotter, J.P. (1996). *Leading Change*. Boston, MA: Harvard Business School Press.

Kotter, J.P. and Heskett, J.L. (2008). *Corporate Culture and Performance*. New York: Free Press.

Kouzes, J.M. and Posner, B.Z. (2017). *The Leadership Challenge*. 6th edn. Hoboken, NJ: Wiley.

Kouzes, J.M. and Posner, B.Z. (2019). 'Leave a Lasting Legacy', *Leadership in Higher Education*, 2(1), pp. 12–18.

Kruse, K. (2015). *Employee Engagement 2.0: How to Motivate Your Team for High Performance (Real-World Strategies That Work)*. CreateSpace Independent Publishing Platform.

Laine, P. and Vaara, E. (2015). 'Participation in Strategy Work: A Bourdieusian Perspective on Organizational Change', *Management*, 18(2), pp. 185–205.

Lencioni, P. (2016). *The Ideal Team Player: How to Recognize and Cultivate the Three Essential Virtues*. Hoboken, NJ: Jossey-Bass.

Lips-Wiersma, M. and Morris, L. (2009). 'Discriminating between "meaningful work" and the "management of meaning"', *Journal of Business Ethics*, 88(3), pp. 491–511. https://doi.org/10.1007/s10551-009-0118-9

Locke, E.A. and Taylor, M.S. (1990). 'Stress, Coping and the Meaning of Work', in Brief, A.P. and Nord, W.R. (eds.) *Meanings of Occupational Work*. Lexington, MA: Lexington Books, pp. 135–170.

Luthans, F., Youssef, C.M. and Avolio, B.J. (2007). *Psychological Capital: Developing the Human Competitive Edge*. Oxford: Oxford University Press.

Maslach, C. and Leiter, M.P. (2016). 'Understanding the burnout experience: recent research and its implications for psychiatry', *World Psychiatry*, 15(2), pp. 103–111. https://doi.org/10.1002/wps.20311WileyOnlineLibrary+1WileyOnlineLibrary+1

McKee, A. (2014). 'It's Time for Companies to Measure People Skills as Carefully as Profits', *Harvard Business Review*, March. Available at: https://hbr.org/2014/03/its-time-for-companies-to-measure-people-skills-as-carefully-as-profits (Accessed: 7 April 2025).

McKinsey and Company. (2021). *Making Work Meaningful from the C-Suite to the Frontline*. Available at: www.mckinsey.com (Accessed: 7 April 2025).

Meadows, D.H. (2008). Thinking in Systems: A Primer. White River Junction, VT: Chelsea Green Publishing.

Meister, J.C. and Willyerd, K. (2010). *The 2020 Workplace: How Innovative Companies Attract, Develop, and Keep Tomorrow's Employees Today*. New York: Harper Business.

Meyer, E. (2014). *The Culture Map: Breaking Through the Invisible Boundaries of Global Business*. New York: PublicAffairs.

Microsoft. (2021). 'Workplace Analytics: Data-Driven Culture and Engagement Insights'. Microsoft. Available at: www.microsoft.com/en-us/worklab/workplace-analytics (Accessed: 1 June 2025).

Microsoft Research (2022). 'Microsoft linked daily tasks to personal growth and connected roles to the company's mission — making meaning real in everyday work.' New Future of Work Report. Microsoft Research. Available at: https://aka.ms/nfw2022 (Accessed: 22 June 2025).

Nooyi, I. (2021). 'Indra Nooyi, former CEO of PepsiCo, on nurturing talent in turbulent times', *Harvard Business Review*, 5 November. Available at: https://hbr.org/2021/11/indra-nooyi-former-ceo-of-pepsico-on-nurturing-talent-in-turbulent-times (Accessed: 15 July 2025).

Obschonka, M., Hakkarainen, K., Lonka, K. and Salmela-Aro, K. (2017). 'Entrepreneurial Legacy: How Leaders Transmit Values Across Generations', *Journal of Business Venturing*, 32(1), pp. 34–51.

Park, N. and Peterson, C. (2008). 'Positive Psychology and Character Strengths: Application to Strengths-Based Organizational Planning', *The Psychologist-Manager Journal*, 11(2), pp. 127–139.

Peck, E. (2017). 'How Culture Drives Performance', Harvard Business Review Digital Articles. Available at: https://hbr.org/2017/01/how-company-culture-shapes-employee-motivation (Accessed: 1 June 2025).

Pink, D.H. (2011). *Drive: The Surprising Truth About What Motivates Us*. Edinburgh: Canongate.

PwC. (2022). 'Hopes and Fears Survey 2022: Workforce Insights'. PwC Global. Available at: www.pwc.com/gx/en/issues/workforce/hopes-and-fears.html (Accessed: 1 June 2025).

PwC. (2024). 'Hopes and Fears Survey 2024: Navigating New Workforce Expectations'. PwC Global. Available at: www.pwc.com/gx/en/issues/work force/hopes-and-fears.html (Accessed: 1 June 2025).

Qualtrics XM Institute. (2022). 'Employee Experience Trends Report 2022'. Qualtrics. Available at: www.qualtrics.com/xm-institute/employee-experince-trends-2022/ (Accessed: 1 June 2025).

Reeve, J., Ryan, R.M., Deci, E.L. and Jang, H. (2018). 'Leader Autonomy Support in the Workplace: A Meta-Analysis', *Journal of Organizational Behavior*, 39(3), pp. 450–468.

Reimer, M., Van Doorne, H. and Van Dyck, C. (2020). 'Legacy in the Making: Building Enduring Cultural Impact', *Journal of Business Strategy*, 41(5), pp. 25–32.

Rosso, B.D., Dekas, K.H. and Wrzesniewski, A. (2010). 'On the Meaning of Work: A Theoretical Integration and Review', *Research in Organizational Behavior*, 30, pp. 91–127.

Rousseau, D.M. (1995). *Psychological Contracts in Organizations: Understanding Written and Unwritten Agreements*. Thousand Oaks, CA: SAGE Publications.

Ryan, L. (2023). *Revolting Women: Why Midlife Women Walk Out, and What to Do About It*. London: Practical Inspiration Publishing.

Ryan, L. (2023). 'The Legacy Lens: Midlife Women and the Meaning of Leadership', *Women & Leadership Studies Quarterly*, 4(1), pp. 14–29.

Saks, A.M. (2006). 'Antecedents and Consequences of Employee Engagement', *Journal of Managerial Psychology*, 21(7), pp. 600–619.

Scharmer, C.O. (2009). *Theory U: Leading from the Future as It Emerges*. San Francisco: Berrett-Koehler.

Schein, E.H. (2010). *Organizational Culture and Leadership*. 4th edn. San Francisco: Jossey-Bass.

Schneider, B., Ehrhart, M.G. and Macey, W.H. (2013). 'Organizational Climate and Culture', *Annual Review of Psychology*, 64, pp. 361–388.

Seligman, M.E.P. (2011). *Flourish: A Visionary New Understanding of Happiness and Wellbeing*. New York: Free Press.

Shamir, B. and Eilam, G. (2005). '"What's your story?" A Life-stories Approach to Authentic Leadership Development', *The Leadership Quarterly*, 16(3), pp. 395–417. https://doi.org/10.1016/j.leaqua.2005.03.005

SHRM. (2022). '2022 State of the Workplace Report: The Changing Expectations of Work and Workers'. Society for Human Resource Management. Available at: www.shrm.org/hr-today/trends-and-forecasting/research-and-surveys/pages/state-of-the-workplace-report-2022.aspx (Accessed: 1 June 2025).

SHRM and Globoforce. (2018). 'The Future of Work is Human'. SHRM and WorkHuman Analytics. Available at: www.workhuman.com/resources/research-report/the-future-of-work-is-human (Accessed: 1 June 2025).

Sinek, S. (2014). *Leaders Eat Last: Why Some Teams Pull Together and Others Don't.* New York: Portfolio.

Sisodia, R., Wolfe, D.B. and Sheth, J.N. (2007). *Firms of Endearment: How World-Class Companies Profit from Passion and Purpose.* Upper Saddle River, NJ: Wharton School Publishing.

Spitzmuller, M. and Stacey, B. (2021). 'Making Purpose Work in Late-career Transitions', *Organizational Dynamics*, 50(4), Article 100826. https://doi.org/10.1016/j.orgdyn.2021.100826

Steger, M.F., Dik, B.J. and Duffy, R.D. (2012). 'Measuring Meaningful Work: The Work and Meaning Inventory (WAMI)', *Journal of Career Assessment*, 20(3), pp. 322–337.

Sutton, R.I. and Rao, H. (2014). *Scaling Up Excellence: Getting to More Without Settling for Less.* New York: Crown Business.

Thompson, J.A. and Bunderson, J.S. (2003). 'Violations of Principle: Ideological Currency in the Psychological Contract', *Academy of Management Review*, 28(4), pp. 571–586.

Ulrich, D. and Ulrich, W. (2010). *The Why of Work: How Great Leaders Build Abundant Organizations That Win.* New York: McGraw-Hill Education.

World Economic Forum (WEF). (2020). 'The Future of Jobs Report 2020'. World Economic Forum. Available at: www.weforum.org/reports/the-future-of-jobs-report-2020 (Accessed: 1 June 2025).

World Economic Forum (WEF). (2025). 'The Future of Jobs Report 2025'. World Economic Forum. Available at: www.weforum.org/reports/future-of-jobs-report-2025 (Accessed: 1 June 2025).

Wheatley, M.J. (2011). *So Far From Home: Lost and Found in Our Brave New World.* San Francisco: Berrett-Koehler.

World Health Organization (WHO). (2019). 'Burn-out an "occupational phenomenon"': International Classification of Diseases. WHO. Available at: www.who.int/news/item/28-05-2019-burn-out-an-occupational-phenomenon-international-classification-of-diseases (Accessed: 1 June 2025).

Wrzesniewski, A., McCauley, C., Rozin, P. and Schwartz, B. (1997). 'Jobs, Careers and Callings: People's Relations to Their Work', *Journal of Research in Personality*, 31(1), pp. 21–33.

Zenger, J.H. and Folkman, J. (2009). *The Inspiring Leader: Unlocking the Secrets of How Extraordinary Leaders Motivate.* New York: McGraw-Hill.

Trademark acknowledgement

Glossary of trademarked terms

Meaning Over Purpose™ – A leadership blueprint for meaningful work. The title and central framework of the book, described in the Introduction as a comprehensive system to embed meaning in an organization and bridge the gap between stated purpose and employees' lived experience. This concept underpins the entire book and integrates all other proprietary models.

Meaning Gap™ – The personal side of the gap. First presented in the Introduction and in dialogues within the book (and also the focus of Appendix 1's self-diagnostic tool), the Meaning Gap refers to the subjective experience of emptiness or lack of meaning in one's work. It's the employee-level manifestation of a purpose-to-meaning disconnect when individuals do not feel that their work matters, despite the organization's stated purpose. Identifying and closing these personal meaning gaps is crucial for engagement and wellbeing.

Purpose-to-Meaning Gap™ – The 'gap' between words and reality. Defined in the Introduction (Figure 1) as the disconnect between an organization's public purpose and the actual meaning employees experience in their daily work. It highlights the shortfall of purpose-alone strategies and sets the stage for why the Meaning Over Purpose approach is needed.

Five Pillars of Meaningful Work™ – Five drivers of employee meaning. Described in the Introduction's outline of the Meaning Over Purpose system (and later detailed in Chapter 5), this framework identifies Autonomy, Mastery, Purpose, Connection and Impact as the fundamental pillars that make work meaningful. Together, they form the foundation of a thriving, engaged workforce.

Lead with Meaning™ – Everyday meaningful leadership. Highlighted in the Introduction as the leadership 'playbook' element of the Meaning Over Purpose blueprint, and expanded in Chapter 7, Lead with Meaning refs to a set of leadership behaviours that infuse daily work with purpose and meaning. It equips leaders to actively model and reinforce the Five Pillars through their actions and decisions, bridging the gap between intent and practice.

Meaning Metrics™ – Measuring what matters. Also mentioned in the Introduction's summary of the blueprint (and detailed in Chapter 8), Meaning Metrics provide a new way to measure culture and meaningful work. By tracking key indicators such as Alignment, Growth, Connection and Resonance, this tool gives quantitative insight into how well an organization is doing in creating meaningful employee experiences, enabling course-correction and evidence-based culture management.

Meaningful Work Ecosystem™ – Embedding meaning at scale. First mentioned in the Introduction's overview of frameworks (and explored in depth in Chapter 6), this model shows that meaningful work is supported by broader systems and culture. It provides a structured approach for leaders to cultivate meaning across all levels of the organization – individual, team, leadership and organizational systems.

Meaningful Work Hexagon™ – Six capabilities for meaningful work. Presented at the close of the Introduction (Figure 3) as the strategic map of the Meaning Over Purpose approach, the Hexagon visual encapsulates six critical capability areas (Purpose and Direction, Personal Meaning, Meaningful Leadership, Meaningful Culture, Measurable Impact and Systemic Sustainability). This integrative model is referenced again in later chapters (e.g., in the book's concluding sections) as a summary of how all components work together to sustain meaningful work at scale.

Meaning Lab™ – An experimental, facilitated team space where leaders and employees collaboratively explore how meaning shows up in their daily work. Used for insight generation, pilot design and systemic reflection during Meaning Over Purpose implementation.

Culture Carriers™ – The systems, stories and rituals that reinforce and protect the desired culture. Culture Carriers help embed meaningful work from the inside out.

Legacy Design Loop™ – A strategic framework for leaders to design their long-term cultural legacy. It integrates legacy visioning, meaning champions, design for sustainability and ongoing renewal, ensuring that meaning endures beyond a single leader or initiative.

Acknowledgements

This book was born from the growing realization that the way we define 'success' in work no longer fits the world we live in. It reflects my belief that work must evolve, from a one-size-fits-all career ladder to something more personalized, human and fulfilling. Meaningful work isn't a luxury; it's a necessity for thriving individuals, resilient organizations and a fairer, more sustainable society.

I want to thank those who stood beside this mission long before it took shape. To the researchers notably Martin Seligman, Scott Barry Kaufman, Adam Grant, Mike Steger, Marjo Lips-Wiersma and Katie Bailey, your work helped legitimize what so many of us feel but struggle to articulate.

To the people-centric leaders and change agents, especially in gender equity and inclusion, who model meaning-driven leadership every day: you are the soul of this movement.

To my MAPPCP (Master's in Applied Positive Psychology and Coaching Psychology) community at the University of East London, and to the wider field of Positive Psychology, thank you for giving me the theoretical scaffolding behind meaningful work, and the courage to integrate what I know with what I feel. As someone who made a midlife career change into entrepreneurship, this programme gave me solid foundations and renewed purpose. You reminded me that enabling people to flourish is not just a noble ideal but a practical, evidence-based strategy.

The seeds of this book were planted through years of navigating my own career, placing bets on jobs, roles and systems that often didn't reflect my values or potential. By turning inward, paying attention to my needs, patterns and passions, I began to understand what I now call 'meaningful work.' That deeply personal process gave me the clarity and conviction to build something bigger than myself.

I have been shaped by wonderful mentors and teachers. In business, June Hicks, Ellen McCarthy, Francis Wood, Peter Baker, Craig Wallace and Tim Gregory. In management and conscious business thought leadership, Marshall Goldsmith, Jack Kornfield, Tara Brach, Tami Simon,

Raj Sisodia, Otto Scharmer and Jeremy Hunter. Each of you taught me lessons in leadership and purpose that have influenced the leader and writer I've become. And to Mr Thompson, my high school English teacher, thank you for unlocking my love of language, writing and encouraging my voice early on.

To the 54 incredible women leaders and entrepreneurs who shared their stories in my research, and to the men, change agents and younger leaders who illuminated the changing needs of the workforce – thank you. Your insights, hopes and challenges are woven through every chapter. To the CEOs, coaches and courageous professionals I've worked with, especially those who struggled to fit into rigid and opaque systems, this is your book too.

To my editor and 'encourager-in-chief' Alison Jones, and everyone at Practical Inspiration Publishing, thank you for your belief and support. To Dr Lucy Ryan, for her inspiration and for connecting me to Alison; and to Dr Ana Paula Nacif, for helping me reveal who I truly am as a coach, your encouragement made all the difference.

To my partner Tony and step-daughter Sophia, thank you for your steadiness and for giving me space to create. To my dear friends and soul sisters, Leonie and Laura. You have both, in different ways, held up mirrors to my strength when I doubted myself. Your belief in me has carried me through my darkest hours, over many years. Thank you from the bottom of my heart.

Index

A quick word from Practical Inspiration Publishing...

We hope you found this book both practical and inspiring – that's what we aim for with every book we publish.

We publish titles on topics ranging from leadership, entrepreneurship, HR and marketing to self-development and wellbeing.

Find details of all our books at: www.practicalinspiration.com

Did you know...

We can offer discounts on bulk sales of all our titles – ideal if you want to use them for training purposes, corporate giveaways or simply because you feel these ideas deserve to be shared with your network.

We can even produce bespoke versions of our books, for example with your organization's logo and/or a tailored foreword.

To discuss further, contact us on info@practicalinspiration.com.

Got an idea for a business book?

We may be able to help. Find out about more about publishing in partnership with us at: bit.ly/PIpublishing.

Follow us on social media...

@PIPTalking

@pip_talking

@practicalinspiration

@piptalking

Practical Inspiration Publishing

www.ingramcontent.com/pod-product-compliance
Lightning Source LLC
Chambersburg PA
CBHW031427270326
41930CB00007B/599